FOUNDATION OF INTELLIGENT IT OPERATIONS

CMDB and Service Maps

**PRAFULL VERMA,
MOHAN KEWALRAMANI,
KALYAN KUMAR**

ACKNOWLEDGEMENT

Ever since I did my first CMDB project in the year 2004-2005, I wanted to share my experience on how easy it is and at the same time how difficult it is. It was built on an asset database. Virtualization was not pervasive like today, in fact virtualization was an insignificant landscape in the whole enterprise IT world. Clouds were non-existent. However, the ITIL hype on CMDB was picking up.

Over a period of next six to seven years years, apart from doing more CMDB projects, I dealt much more on clarifying the misconceptions about CMDB and educating IT folks on the subject, as the enterprise IT landscape also evolved with virtualization and clouds. The idea of publishing this book thus materialized.

This project would not have been successful without the encouragement and support from my wife Annie and daughter Naomi who adjusted to my working at odd hours of the day and being appreciative of my application.

I am also thankful to my colleagues who, directly and indirectly helped in brainstorming and providing inputs.

Prafull Verma

Acknowledgement from Co-Authors

I would like to thank my wife Maisa, who has made this and everything else possible for me. She has truly been the enabler for everything that I have experienced, learnt and achieved. Also, my two boys, Zaahid and Aariz, for always keeping me grounded. I would also like to thank Shafiq, for setting me on the path of Service Management, it has been a fun journey!

Everything that I have learnt, has been at the time and expense of all the customers that I have had the opportunity to work with, I sincerely thank them, as without them, none of this would have been possible. Last, but not the least, all of my colleagues at HCL, who I have learnt a lot from.

Mohan Kewalramani

Ever Since my exposure the world of CMDB and its previous ancestors this has always been a complex area for the entire value chain to understand and be able to lookup to a practical/pragmatic approach to get this implemented. Rather than making it a Unicorn of the mythical world, we want to make it a race horse of the real world.

I would like to thank my wife Zulfia and Son Azlan who have given me the space and time out of their share to enable me to write this book and always inspire me in pushing the limits and also acting like a sounding board for simplifying the thoughts

Kalyan Kumar

FOREWORD

"Yesterday I was clever, so I wanted to change the world. Today I am wise, so I am changing myself."

— Rumi

The digital revolution is changing the world around us every day and bringing new digital services for the consumers and businesses alike. Powered by new micro services, dynamic infrastructure, cloud computing, and mobile access have provided great agility and flexibility to organizations that can leverage these technologies to provide differentiated services to their employees, business partners and customers. However these digital services do not exist by themselves they often require a great deal of interconnectivity to legacy and mainstream services. Over the last five decades as the IT computing paradigms have evolved, the complexity of business services and the applications and infrastructure that support them has grown bigger and more complex. This complexity has made performance, availability and compliance ever more challenging.

More than ever organizations rely on the agility and flexibility of their IT infrastructure and services for competitive advantage to bring new digital services to market and manage existing services with the highest availability, reliability and efficiency. The solution to this necessary mandate is better processes, organizational structure with well defined roles and technology solutions that are designed to integrate, automate and manage the hybrid enterprise.

One of the key enabling technologies for this revolution is a Configuration Management Database (CMDB), which provides configuration information for many of these new and old processes. Over the last decade many organizations have implemented CMDB/CMS technologies to address one or more IT service management processes. Often these deployments faced challenges in data accuracy, scope of data and other environmental and organizational factors, which often limit the value of the technology.

This book collects a set of best practices to address and overcome some of the design and deployment challenges with ITSM and CMDB and can help unlock the true value of an enterprise CMDB in your organization. The author uses experience from hundreds of deployments to provide a practical, pragmatic, and detailed approach for how to achieve success in design, implementation and the operations of a federated enterprise CMDB/CMS. Towards the end of the book the author provides prescriptive guidelines on how to take advantage of the CMDB to design and model Business Services which are essential to managing the digital enterprise.

Kia Behnia

Startup Advisor & Incubator,
Former CTO of BMC Software

TABLE OF CONTENTS

1 INTRODUCTION

The scale of Enterprise IT environments is growing rapidly and computing resources are deployed in abundance. Consequently, management of IT operations to keep the lights on and to achieve the desired level of services needs to be scaled up significantly. Though the growth of computing resources is exponential, the corresponding growth in traditional operations management functions cannot scale up exponentially. A critical part of operations is to "keep the lights on"; that is to ensure that there is no interruption or disruption in the IT services provided and if any unplanned interruptions were to occur, then identifying the correct point of failure and rectifying it as quickly as possible, as well as preventing the chain reaction due to the failure. In most organizations, millions of components are interconnected across complex networks and a certain amount of intelligence is required to be able to make decisions about what actions should be taken and where.

Intelligence in government operations as well as in business operations are of paramount importance and play a vital role for their success. Operating any of these organizations without an intrinsic understanding of internal as well as external influencing factors would never be considered. It is no different when successfully and efficiently running IT operations. It is vital to have an understanding of the discrete components, their individual and collective properties in relation to other discrete components that will enable operations professionals to deal with ongoing or potential issues. IT operations, like business operations, needs the ability to learn or understand the structure of the environment, their dependencies on each other as well as how to deal with new and/or difficult situations. Service Maps and the CMDB (Configuration Management Database) are key tools for intelligent operations. Some of the drivers for the need of this intelligence are:

Complexity of IT landscape:

Figure 1 depicts the growth in complexity in the IT landscape since the era of dumb terminals to the modern era of cloud computing. It is not just the complexity of the whole landscape but the complexity of individual CI (Configuration items) that is also rapidly growing. In order to manage such a complex IT landscape, you would need to manage the individual components' as well, as it has potential to impact the overall landscape due to dependencies between all of the different components. One simple example of how IT components have evolved is to compare *"Windows 95"* – the default operating system client in the client server era vs the *"Windows 8"* operating system now. After booting a *Windows 95* laptop, if you were to run the task manager, you would probably find less than twenty processes running. However, if you check the number of processes running on a Windows 8 laptop, it would likely be over 50.

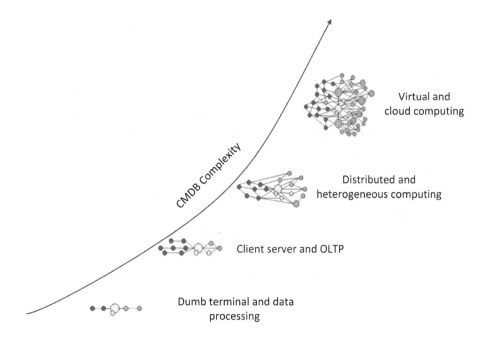

Figure 1: Growing Complexity

Growing scale of specialized components in the landscape

Another important aspect is a shifting of multipurpose components to point products that fulfil a specific purpose and this is applicable to components in both the hardware as well as software areas. You will find many specialized software in the form of utilities and plug-ins for a very specific purpose. Load balancing, identity management, orchestration services are some examples.

When ITIL introduced the concepts of CMDB in ITIL v2 in 2002, it was primarily for the consideration of client server computing and heterogeneous computing. Cloud computing was non-existent in that era.

Diversified technology integration

Earlier, IT as an enterprise was segregated into a front office IT function and back office IT. In several industries it was also the segregation of business IT with enterprise IT. Now, the consumerism of technology has blurred many of these boundaries. Consumerism as a culture, was typically applied to enterprise IT, for example – "an app store in the workplace domain". Due to the invasion of mobile devices and innovation in other technical/electrical products, users are now more familiar with using technology, features and functions as soon as it is developed and released. This phenomenon has created the need of integration between diversified technologies. With a mobile device in my hand I want to approve or reject a request by gesture, just like I control my TV by gesture rather than by remote!

Dependency of the business on IT

Business complexity is growing and to deal with this complexity, business looks to technology. Software engineering has changed the business world. We have software for almost every business problem. The irony is that the growth in the complexity of software is much higher than the growth in the business itself. That means, whenever IT solves a business problem, it creates another internal problem that it has to deal with. The resolution of a business problem is shifted into additional IT problems, or, the complexity is multiplied and introduced in the IT world. When you have an internal business problem to solve, that typically springs up another IT solution or IT Information system – the CMDB and service maps are core parts of that solution. This reminds me of other paradoxes - We are drowning in data, but starved for knowledge. We have lots of data, but no real information. It is similar to the irony of our world - People are living longer, but that does not mean that people are living healthier?

1.1 CMDB and Service Maps in Knowledge Hierarchy

Figure 2 shows the DIKW (Data, Information, Knowledge and Wisdom) hierarchy and how CMDB and Service maps fall within that hierarchy.

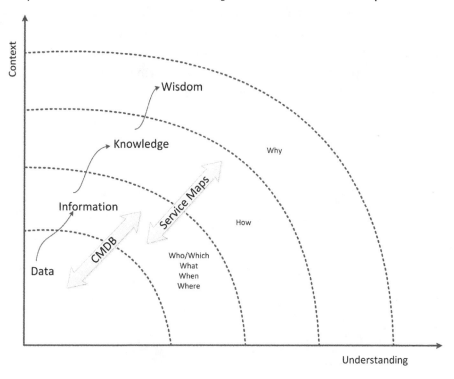

Figure 2: CMDB and Service maps in DIKW hierarchy

Data is the collection of facts from which conclusions may be drawn. Information is the data with context and perspective. Knowledge is the information with guidance for actions based upon insight and experience. CMDB is thus, the data as well as some information, while service maps are built on top of the CMDB and therefore a service map forms the information and knowledge.

The purpose of this book

This book is written for IT generalists as well as IT Service Management professionals. The purpose is to educate IT generalists with the basics of a CMDB and service maps without any need to understand the technology or any specialist tools. This book is also intended to guide IT service management professionals to build an intelligent information system that produce real benefits and to support the management of IT services by having a reliable and enriched source of information, that will radically help in making better decisions.

2 CMDB: WHERE DID IT COME FROM?

ITIL introduced the concept of a CMDB (Configuration Management Data Base) more than two decades ago and it formed the core, supporting most of the other processes, yet many organizations are still not sure if they have implemented it correctly within their organizations. The primary reason is that along with the concept of the CMDB, ITIL though inadvertently, also brought in many misconceptions around the CMDB as well. *"Experts"* and software vendors attempted to expand that even further and soon the CMDB hype was created. Although the hype has mostly faded away, but the effects are still visible, which begs the question – *"has the organization built the CMDB correctly"*? In this book, we try to share our experiences and opinion around this subject.

The difference between the "theoretical" and "practical reality" of a CMDB, as professionals learn from books and what they actually see in their professional lives can be well explained by an anecdote that a friend once cited to me. To a group of people, he asked *"Does anyone know what a Unicorn is"*? Everyone, as expected, knew the legendary animal. He proceeded to then ask them to draw a picture of what a Unicorn looks like. Everyone drew the picture and they were unanimous on the fact that a Unicorn is a horse with a large, pointed, spiraling horn projecting from its forehead. Then he asked the question – *"has anyone seen a Unicorn"*? The answer obviously from everyone in the group was that they hadn't. This is exactly what the situation is with a CMDB in the IT industry for a very long time. Everyone who reads or studies the ITIL book knew what a CMDB was, but none had actually seen one.

What do you expect from a CMDB?

This is the by far the most important question you need to get answers to, before embarking on or sponsoring any CMDB project. Keep away from the hype that has largely been created by vendors and a few research analysts. We intend to give you our views on what you *should* expect from a CMDB.

CMDB is a database and its usefulness depends largely on your requirements and expectations from it, what data you hold and how you use that data. To give you an analogy, let's look at a geography map, say "Google maps". Its use is based on the data about the geography, the places within that geography and how these places are connected or located in respect to each other. The value you obtain from the map depends upon:

1. The richness and the quality of the information available in the map or displayed in the map.

2. Your own capability to use that information for example, use it for a specific application, driving directions.

Additionally, you can obtain additional information from other sources and overlay that on the map and use it for even other purposes, for example to locate a restaurant, or traffic congestion and the quickest route to your destination.

Similarly, a CMDB is a database that can hold data and information. It does not provide knowledge and will not perform any functions by itself. It is the responsibility of the user of a CMDB to make it useful. Depending on your use cases and the information you expect to derive from a CMDB will dictate the type and the richness of the data that will be required to be held in the CMDB.

It is also important to note that just populating the data in the CMDB is not sufficient, it is critical to ensure that the accuracy of the data is maintained. There is little point in holding data if you cannot rely on it when you need to make decisions based on the information it provides.

2.1 Evolution of CMDB with ITSM tools

You may notice we have made frequent references to ITIL V2 in this book. The reason for this is that "CMDB" as a term is used in ITIL V2, whereas ITIL refers to it as a CMS. Refer to section 2.2 of this book, where the differences have been compared. Our belief is that from a service management knowledge and guidance perspective, the ITIL V2 book set is significantly stronger than ITIL V3. If you draw a comparison this to the software world, ITIL V2 is extremely strong in terms of business logic and algorithms, but doesn't provide a fancy user interface. Whereas ITIL V3 is exactly the opposite, where the user interface is very pretty and provides a good user experience, but there isn't a lot under the hood.

Until the year 2003, there was no built in CMDB in any commercial off the shelf ITSM tool, nevertheless I would say that the CMDB's predecessor did actually exist in the form of an Asset DB in early ITSM tools. Peregrine for example, a very popular ticketing system started the concept of every incident being related to one or more asset items. It was very simple and it worked extremely well, because the ability of one component impacting the larger landscape was limited due to the simple landscape. As the complexity of the IT infrastructure grew, middleware, intranet, clusters, virtualization, distributed application etc. became a routine part of the IT Infrastructure; the need for information regarding the complex relationships became imminent. The benefits of the CMDB being the provider of this information was perceived very well. As the popularity of ITIL V2 grew, it promoted the concepts of the CMDB and a clear market demand emerged that was soon capitalized on by ITSM tool vendors. The CMDB became an integral part of every ITSM tool.

The DMTF (Distributed Management Task Force) took on the initiative to standardize a Common Information Model. The DMTF is a not-for-profit association of industry members dedicated to promoting enterprise and systems management and their interoperability. The DMTF's Common Information Model (CIM) provides a common definition of management information for systems, networks, applications and services, and allows for extensions to vendor systems and information sharing. This standard soon became a reference model and tool vendors built their CMDB data model based on this model.

Today we don't only see the CMDB as an integral part of ITSM tools but also other supporting data management tools such as discovery tools, working in a seamless manner and exchanging data with one another as a part of the ITSM ecosystem with the CMDB sitting at the core.

2.2   CMDB vs CMS vs CMDBf

The literal difference by definition is of a database vs a system. A database means a collection of information, whereas a system refers to a regularly interacting or interdependent group of items forming a unified whole.

CMDB is terminology from ITIL V2 and perceived as a *single* large database, although not explicitly stated. CMS is terminology from ITIL V3, where it is explicitly stated as a distributed system and inherently federated. The scope of a CMS is considered to be quite large. The CMDB slowly graduated towards a CMDBf (Federated CMDB), where data was physically held in disparate databases and federated to the CMDB and eventually to a CMS. The term CMDB remains alive but is now considered to be what essentially a MDR (Management Data Repository) is. In a CMDBf and CMS, a MDR is a basic collection of CIs and their relationships, which form a self-contained entity within the CMS hierarchy. It is deemed to be a member of a CMDBf.

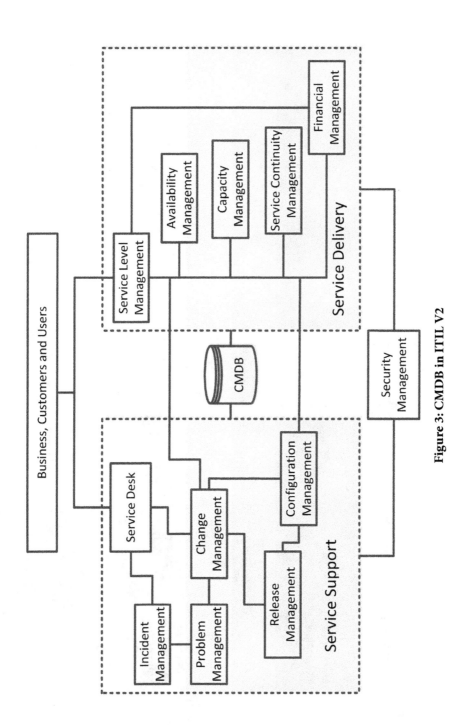

Figure 3: CMDB in ITIL V2

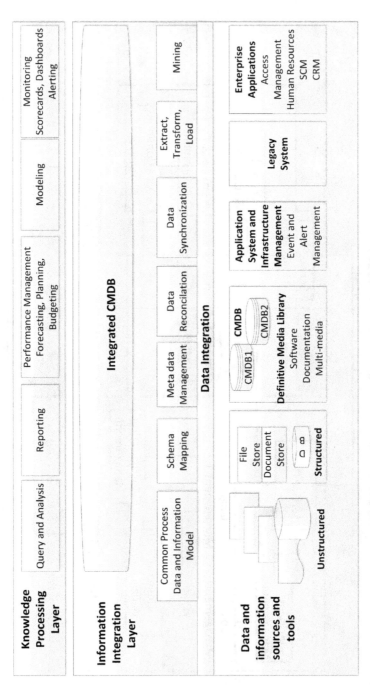

Figure 4: CMS in ITIL V3

ITIL V3 has made the scope of the CMS so broad, that it is most likely to remain theoretical and on paper. It would be the *Unicorn* that everyone knows, but never seen. In fact, ITIL also does not differentiate between a CMS and a SKMS (Service Knowledge Management System). According to ITIL, both are exactly the same - just replace the title of the "integrated CMDB" box in *figure 4* with "*Service Knowledge Management System*" and the entire system becomes a SKMS. Refer to the ITIL V3 service transition book (ISBN 978-0-11-331048-7), Figure 4.8 on page 68 that represents the diagram of a CMS and Figure 4.39 on page 151 that represents the diagram of a SKMS. It is a no brainer to realize that both are exactly the same except for the title of one box.

CMDBf

CMDBf is an acronym that stands for Configuration Management Database Federation. The CMDBf was an industry consortium formed in 2006 to develop a specification for CMDB federation. The consortium was not affiliated with any standards organization. The CMDBf published a specification in October 2007. The CMDBf consortium then donated the specification to the DMTF, and the CMDBf consortium was officially dissolved. The DMTF CMDB Federation Working Group was then formed to shepherd the consortium specification through the DMTF standards acceptance process. The DMTF published the standard in June 2009.

CMDBf, as the acronym suggest, relies on using data federation to build a purposeful CMDB and provides a practical way to achieve the goals of a CMS. Federation presents some or all data from different data sources as if it were stored in a single virtual data store. The member databases of a federated database usually maintain independent control of the data they contain.

These member data sources are called Management Data Repositories (MDRs). A similar result of a centralized view can be achieved in a limited way, by periodically loading data from the MDRs to the CMDB through *Extract, Transform*, and *Load* (ETL) technology. ETL does present some problems because data stored in multiple places can become stale and out of sync between data transfers. Increasing the frequency of transfers or even initiating a transfer in real time with every change may diminish the issue of stale data, but, the additional overhead for transfer can be considerable. In a federated system, the CMDB queries the MDR for data when it is needed by the CMDB, thereby always presenting the user with up to date information from the remote data source.

Figure 5 depicts and architectural overview of a CMDBf. Each member MDR will have their own methods to collect and maintain data. Push mode of data federation requires implementation of a registration service at the CMDBf, while a pull mode of data federation requires implementing a query service at the MDR. Push-mode federation has the advantage of simplicity and improved query performance, however it has the disadvantage that data may be pushed to the CMDB even when it is not needed. The advantage with a pull-mode federation is that data is transported only when a client queries it, or a CMDB wishes to refresh its cache, however it has the disadvantage that a user may have to wait for the information requested from the CMDBf as queries may take longer to execute, due to the real time request/refresh nature of the architecture and the performance issue of gathering data from remote data sources. The query service serves a similar role as a SQL database query service, but the CMDBf query service does not rely on the use of SQL or an RDBMS, it also provides a way to aggregate data from multiple repositories and contains additional special support for graph queries.

A Federated CMDB may also pull some of the data from non-traditional data sources like infrastructure management tools or have its own method to collect and maintain data directly from infrastructure discovery tools.

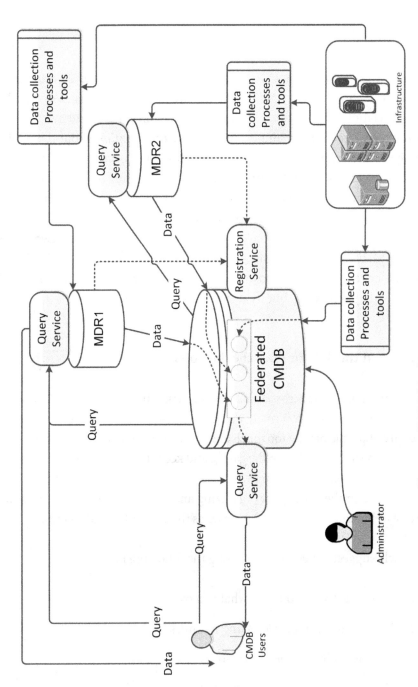

Figure 5: CMDBf Architecture overview

2.3   CMDB cost vs benefits

In the early era prior to the ITIL CMDB idea being introduced, IT continued to function well without a CMDB. The need for a CMDB emerged due to the complex relationships between IT components (configuration items) and the ongoing requirement for maintaining accurate ***information*** about these relationships. I am emphasizing the word "information", because, I differentiate between "information" and "data". Data may not have any meaning or associated interpretation whereas that is not the case with information, which does have meaning and associated interpretation. Information is derived from data and in many contexts it is implied or self-derived. I do still use these two words interchangeably with the assumption that data has the required implied information. I have observed one common weakness across many implemented CMDB's – they store data, but treat that as information.

Do you own the data or does the data own you?

A long time ago, I came across an interesting article in the New York Times that talked of people having too many things. It spoke about the general tendency and desire of people having too much and wanting even more. When we run out of space in the house, we fill up the garage and keep the car out to make space for other things!! When we hold on to stuff we no longer want, need or use, there is a hidden cost, in the time spent organizing and contemplating use of the stuff. The cost of holding these things increases as the amount of stuff increases.

The article suggested people think along the following lines:

1.   Why exactly do you own what you own?

2.   What could you get rid of and not miss?

3.   Do you really still need that stuff?

4.   What is it costing you to own that?

The tendency to possess a lot of stuff leads to being possessed by holding on to it and the desire for more never ends. It is not only a cruel cycle, but insane as well.

Well, the analogy applies to the amount of data in the CMDB too. Many organizations own and hold enormous amounts of data, assuming that it will someday be required. They spend lots of time and efforts (and therefore costs) to collect, store and manage that data but do not critically evaluate the value of this data and continue to own and manage that data, even when it is no longer useful. Data never gets deleted. There is a hidden cost of holding data in the CMDB. While we understand the benefits of a CMDB, a common mistake is to misunderstand the value of the CMDB. Value is the ratio of the benefit and cost. Therefore the value will determine the cost justifiable benefits. A CMDB is an investment for the better management of the infrastructure and therefore the services derived out from that infrastructure. Figure 4 provides the value curve of a typical CMDB. This depicts the three zones

Zone 1- the point of entry

The initial zone or the point of entry – within this zone the benefit realization may or may not be very appealing or encouraging. However, this stage is unavoidable and the primary reason for the increased cost and effort is the initial set up and the foundation costs that will come with any CMDB project.

Zone 2 – the value zone

The cost justifiable benefits of CMDB lie here. The benefits rise appreciably with optimal cost increase. The returns on the investments are maximum in this zone.

Zone 3- the maturity zone

The maturity rises, delivering a higher quantity, quality and increased accuracy of CMDB data and the derivative information, but there is also a steep rise in costs to achieve this level. The return on investments may not be very appealing in this zone, but the criticality of the information provided by the CMDB to the business may still justify the costs.

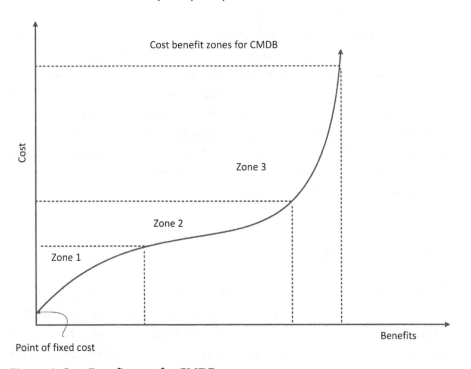

Figure 6: Cost Benefit zone for CMDB

2.3.1   CMDB Costs

Like all other projects of this nature, CMDB costs can be allocated to two primary areas – building the CMDB and the ongoing maintenance of it. The build stage will deal with the initial costs of the technology, the efforts required to set up the CMDB and creating a baseline, whist the run stage will then deal with data maintenance – ensuring that data is updated and provides the benefits and value expected from it.

Setting up the CMDB

A meaningful CMDB project should consist of at least 3 elements

1. Design – the data model and CMDB architecture, which will be driven by the requirements that the CMDB is expected to fulfil. The data model has been described in section 3.3.2 of this book.

2. CMDB baseline creation – Identify the various multiple data sources that will feed into the CMDB, data discovery and collection via discovery tools and manual methods, data preparation and data loading

3. Control process design and implementation

There is a general perception that discovery tools do everything that is required to build a CMDB. This is not true at all. I have come across several organizations, whose CMDB implementation only comprised of using discovery tools and populating whatever data it was able to provide into the CMDB. Customers couldn't derive any value out of these implementations and turned to us to procure consulting services to fix the issue of their CMDB not serving the intended purpose. Discovery is a vital, albeit very small part of a real CMDB project, but it isn't a CMDB implementation on its own. To give your CMDB project the greatest chance of success and for it to deliver the value expected from a CMDB, the typical areas that will require commercial investment to set it up right are:

1. Consulting cost to design the data model, CMDB and discovery tools architecture, control processes and ongoing maintenance procedures

2. Licenses for discovery tools

3. Professional services to implement the discovery tools

4. Hardware costs to host the discovery tools

5. Resource efforts for data collection and data preparation

6. CMDB tool (most probably contained within the ITSM tool) configuration

7. Professional services to implement the control processes

8. Training

9. And of course, the project management cost

The commercial investment would depend on multiple factors such as:

- The size of the environment, which would directly impact the cost of discovery in terms of the number of licenses and the effort required for deployment of discovery capabilities

- The size also determines the amount of data that needs to be discovered, overlaid with other data, processed, stored and managed

- The CMDB design – some of the data elements could warrant significant efforts to gather and validate

- Depth and width of the CMDB

Maintaining the CMDB

The amount of investment and effort required for maintaining the data currency and accuracy should not be underestimated. In the build phase, control processes are designed and implemented for data maintenance. These controls include the data updates by automated (e.g. via discovery tools) as well as manual methods. The typical areas that will incur costs for maintaining a CMDB usually encompass:

1. The cost of managing the deployed tools and the processes for automation

2. Costs for staff that data update via manual methods (every data element cannot be discovered and maintained by automated approaches)

3. The cost of auditing and correcting deviations identified in the CMDB

4. Regular enhancements, addition of new CI attributes, new data sources, reporting, induction of new staff, etc.

2.3.2 CMDB benefits

Any information by itself does not deliver any benefit, unless you use the information to fulfill a purpose. The benefit is determined by how you use it. A CMDB thus provides you with information that could lead to the path of wisdom and enhance your capabilities for supporting and running the business. Several of the benefits can be quantified, but it is not necessary to quantify each and every benefit. The "quality" factor provided by the CMDB in supporting better decision making and understanding dependencies is not easily quantifiable. Some of the use cases where a CMDB would justify its existence would be:

1. A CMDB is the most powerful tool to plan a change, assess the risk of a change and avoid change failures.

2. The CMDB is the key information provider to build and maintain the service continuity plan.

3. The CMDB is the key data provider for the event management process, to enable event correlation and rapid response

4. The CMDB is the key data provider for incident management and problem management for incident and problem analysis

5. The CMDB is the data provider for calculating the cost of service and financial management

6. The CMDB is the information provider for availability management and capacity/performance management- both of which are the foundation for BSM (Business Service Management)

7. CMDB enables building of service maps and service models and therefore BSM

IT service delivery and support staff may know their own MDR extremely well as they deal with the components in their area of responsibility on a daily basis, but working in isolation or working on tribal knowledge is no longer an option due to the complex nature of IT environments and the intricate dependency and relationships between all the components and form part of the service chains. Even services are dependent on other services to fulfil an end to end function. The CMDB should be the authorized source of information for supporting all service management activities.

An example of the proven value of a CMDB

The SAP landscape is an extremely complex environment and has proven the value of CMDB for landscape management.

SAP Solution manager is the service management tool for SAP environments and SLD – System Landscape Directory the predecessor of LMDB – Landscape Management Database, is the CMDB for SAP environment. LMDB has demonstrated enormous value to support the complex SAP environment and its value is undisputable.

SAP solution manager and SAP SLD/LMDB are the most important tools used to manage these complex environments. No SAP customer can even dream of managing their SAP landscape and application lifecycle without these two supporting tools for SAP.

ITIL CMDB has in fact got its inspiration for these concepts from SAP and have since been trying to emulate that in the form of a CMDB for the entire IT landscape.

2.4 Different Aspects of CMDB
Depth and width of CMDB

Figure 7 below illustrates the aspects of "depth" and the "width" of a CMDB. The depth refers to the layers of the environment, while the width refers to the number of CI's included in the CMDB.

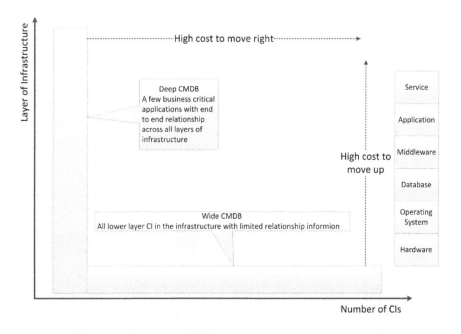

Figure 7: Depth and width of CMDB

It is easier to obtain data about the lower layer of the infrastructure because most of this data can be discovered relatively easily using discovery tools, which if given the right level of access, can run certain commands and gather all sorts of hardware, software and relationship information. However, the need for gathering data manually rises as you go up to the upper layers of the infrastructure. As a general rule the cost of moving right at the lower level is relatively low when compared to the cost of moving up. The cost multiplier is the multiplication of depth and the width.

Enterprise IT organizations are normally structured to attain efficiency at the horizontal level, usually based on the technology layer. Therefore a "wide" CMDB will be useful for infrastructure management across all services. A "deep" CMDB is extremely useful if the enterprise IT service delivery organization structure is based on vertical business functions, for example in the financial services industry, the mortgage service IT typically has its own end to end stack to manage the service.

Sensible CMDB

A sensible CMDB is the optimal combination of depth and width taking into account multiple considerations, including the costs and ROI.

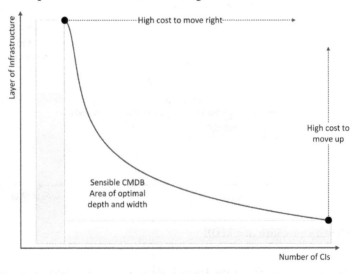

Figure 8: Sensible CMDB

What should be the optimal depth and width (or the right size) is determined by various requirements and would be different for different organizations. This requires a detailed analysis of the environment and the needs of consumers of the data in the CMDB. The size of the CMDB has a direct impact on the accuracy and the currency of data. The cost and efforts required to maintain the currency and the accuracy greatly depend on the size of the CMDB. Technical feasibility is yet another criteria. With the availability of modern technology, nothing is impossible. (Technically, it is also feasible for anybody to walk on the moon, if you have the money for it.) The decisions are more a commercial decision, rather than a technical one.

A federated CMDB (CMDBf) is probably the only practical answer to enable the scalability of a CMDB while still keeping it sensible.

2.5 Misconception about CMDB

Based on our varied experiences spanning many customers, we have come across several common misconceptions or misunderstanding about a CMDB that we would like to highlight and also provide our views on it:

CMDB is a centralized database

Somehow, ITIL V2 created this perception that the CMDB was a large, single centralized database, but that isn't true. Several organizations have built their CMDB in the form of a centralized database within their ITSM tool's CMDB module. For a small sized organization, a centralized database may be feasible, but for most large organizations, especially those that would warrant the existence of a CMDB for their efficient functioning, a CMDB as a central database wouldn't scale up for the real world requirement for an organization of their size. A CMDB would usually be a set of multiple databases. What is normally created is a centralized view so that all data can be viewed holistically instead of than in isolation, rather than a centralized database.

ITIL provides well-defined guidelines for content in a CMDB

This is also unfortunately not true. ITIL V2 has provided fairly detailed guidance on the configuration management process and also *suggests* 24 attributes for a CI. (Refer annex 7C of Service Support- ISBN 0-11-330015-8). This is however far from what is really required to build a meaningful CMDB that will deliver any real use and value.

Additionally, ITIL also creates a perception that everything that exists in the IT environment should be held in the CMDB. It also explicitly states that documents should be held as a CI. Our strong recommendation is that only data that actually adds any value to you should be held. It is just not practical to hold documents as a CI in the real world. Most organizations use some form of a document management system to manage their important documents. Is the document management system then a CMDB or MDR or does it become irrelevant because this information will instead be held in the CMDB?

It is important to remember that collecting, storing and maintaining data has a cost! If you don't need it, don't hold it. We have discussed a "sensible" CMDB in the previous section as well as the cost considerations as you increase the depth or width or even the CI types that you decided to hold in the CMDB.

CMDB is a single source of truth

If a CMDB is not a centralized database, then it also cannot be a single source of truth. It certainly does have the potential to be the single source of truth.

The CMDB inherits the integrity from multiple data sources or suppliers and it is only reliable if all the data sources provide accurate and complete data. Therefore, by making sure the suppliers of the data provide truthful data, you could make the CMDB as the consolidated source of truth.

Configuration management process and CMDB

Another common scenario that we have seen on several occasions is the sheer pride from IT organizations in regards to their CMDB implementation. We must not forget that the CMDB is a database and without a configuration management process, it will soon be out of date whereby it would have no value. What is the point of collecting and holding data if you cannot trust it when you need it most?

In almost all cases, we have observed that their CMDB implementations were actually deployment of a tool, or in some cases multiple tools, but no process. The CMDB and configuration management are not the same. The CMDB is a database, while configuration management is the control process built around the CMDB to maintain the accuracy, currency and integrity of the data in the CMDB.

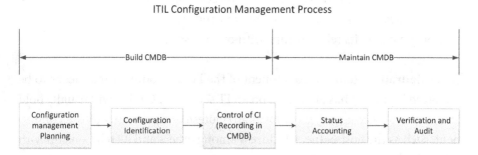

Figure 9: ITIL Configuration Management

We split the ITIL configuration management process into two parts – "build" and "maintain" as they map to the project and operations stages respectively.

Further, in this book, we have also discussed the configuration management process as the data maintenance process. Since data maintenance is primarily controlled by the change management process, we could also consider the change management process as the primary control for the configuration management process.

2.6   Asset Management and CMDB

The term "asset management", is very commonly used for hardware asset management and most people consider the CMDB a part of asset management. Technically speaking, asset management includes hardware asset management as well as software asset management, but an Asset and a CI are two different things.

2.6.1   Asset versus CI versus a managed object

An asset is a hardware product or a software license that needs to be managed, because it has some *economic value.* An asset DB is the database that holds and provides information about IT assets. An asset DB will contain information about *economic attributes* such as the cost, depreciation, contract details, renewal dates, purchase order information and the purchase date but *no* information regarding its relationships with other assets.

A configuration item is a component of the IT environment that needs to be managed because it has an impact on an IT service. A CMDB will usually hold information regarding the technical attributes/configurations of the component, such as the host name, IP address among others and its relationship with other CIs, but *no* information about its economic value.

An asset may or may not be a CI; conversely, a CI may or may not be an asset. Asset DBs and CMDBs may share some common items—for example, data center devices—but the information (attributes) that they will hold for these items will differ. Some items may be included only in an asset DB but not in the CMDB: for example, end-user devices and software licenses.

Some items may be included only in a CMDB but not in an asset DB: for example, a logical system (cluster and virtual machine but note—in cloud computing, a virtual machine is a candidate for asset item as well).

The Asset life cycle is also significantly longer. For example, a server can exist in the asset DB in the status of "in stock," but will not appear in a CMDB until the server has actually been provisioned, in which case within the asset DB, the status transits to "deployed"; similarly, a decommissioned asset will not exist in a CMDB but will exist in an asset DB.

The asset management process and the configuration-management processes are not the same. The Asset management process is the **control process** built around an *asset DB* and deals with accounting, purchasing, depreciation and disposal processes. Configuration management is the control process built around the *CMDB* and deals with technical configuration changes, such as port change or addition/removal of memory or storage, route change and changes in its relationship to other CI's.

Figure 10 below depicts the relationship between assets, CI's and managed objects.

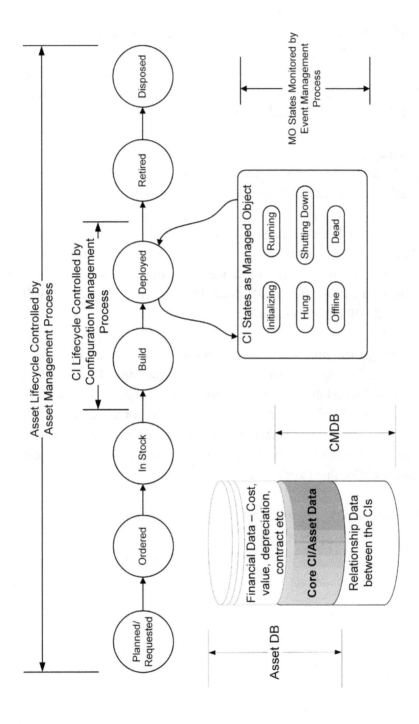

Figure 10: Asset, CI and Managed Object relation

Asset discovery is *not* part of the asset management process. Typical asset management proposals for implementation (excluding software asset management) will contain two primary elements:

1. Creation of an asset DB

2. Development and implementation of an asset management process

While the first part is a simpler activity, the second part is much more complex as compared to the configuration management process. The cost of implementing the asset management process is significantly higher than the cost of the tools/ technology typically used. The typical asset life cycle includes the following:

1. Procuring of IT assets

   a. Identifying requirements

   b. Initiating the IT asset procurement service

   c. Processing procurement information requests

   d. Processing IT asset requests

   e. Issuing purchase orders and tracking invoices

2. Receiving IT assets

   a. Asset tag generation

   b. Managing the IT asset inventory

   c. Updating the IT asset inventory

   d. Performing / auditing inventory

   e. Resolving inventory exceptions

3. Managing IT asset operations

   a. Monitoring IT asset operations (e.g., install, maintain, support)

    b.   Handling IT asset hardware lifecycle events (changes, upgrades, etc.)

    c.   Warranties and maintenance contracts

    d.   Asset refresh planning

4. Managing IT asset accounting

    a.   Depreciation and value tracking

    b.   Charge back

    c.   Managing accounts payable

5. Returning / Disposing IT assets

    a.   Decommissioning assets

    b.   Preparing IT assets for return or disposal

    c.   Returning IT assets

    d.   Disposing IT assets

A comprehensive asset management process will serve a variety of goals and you need to focus on your goals. If your goal is controlling the CAPEX (capital expenditure), focus on the first sub process; if your goal is good service delivery; focus on the third and fourth sub processes. If your goal is controlling OPEX (operating expenditure), focus on the fifth sub process; and if you want compliance, then focus on the third and fifth sub process.

If the scope of your asset management project includes software as well, keep in mind that software asset management is very complex and comprehensive and typically includes the following:

1. Selection, standardization, and approval for software products (especially architectural and compatibility consideration in the environment)

2. Purchasing or otherwise obtaining software, such as downloading it for use

3. Managing software installations, licenses, and contracts, including proof of ownership (this ends up being very complex because of the wide variety of licensing schemes, such as pay-by-use, install based, processor or core based which relies on the hardware it is installed on or other kinds of end user license agreements (ELA))

4. Reclaiming licensed software for reuse (harvesting process)

5. Creating and maintaining a definitive software library (DSL)

6. Legal compliance and preventing unauthorized use

Many real world asset management software implementations usually only address a part of the above processes. A colleague, who has spent most of his professional life helping organizations implement software asset management processes and technology once told me about a financial services client in the UK that he had dealt with. They had struggled for years, trying to conquer the asset management process and get it to deliver any tangible benefits. It was just too hard. Eventually they came up with an interesting solution. For every 100 pounds they spent on software, they put aside an additional 10% to pay the vendor as a penalty when and if they got audited. They found this an easier approach, rather than implementing a working software asset management process and its related controls. Of course, they were assuming that the penalty would be equal or under the 10% they were setting aside and lower than the cost of implementing a software asset management process, which is never the case.

2.6.2 Asset DB Vs CMDB

An Asset DB and CMDB can broadly be compared as:

ASSET DB	CMDB
Simple database, Complex process	Complex database, simple process
Involved in the overall lifecycle of every IT asset, even if not yet deployed	Involves assets that are deployed in the IT environment for active use
Financial Data – Cost, Value, Depreciation, Contract etc.	Core CI, Relationship Data between CI's
Maintains more non-technical information	Maintains technical information of CI
Monitored via asset inventory with various statuses	Monitored via the event management process
Asset lifecycle controlled by asset management process	CI lifecycle controlled by configuration management process

Asset management is a very large, separate subject and this book does not discuss it.

2.7 *Typical Enterprise IT Environment*

As depicted in Figure 11, contemporary enterprise IT infrastructure is a complex mesh of multiple systems that include

1. Traditional IT Infrastructure in distributed datacenters

2. Virtual infrastructure and private cloud built over traditional infrastructure with multiple independent vendors such as MS Azure and VMware

3. Business application software

4. Enterprise applications

5. Multiple public clouds – IaaS, PaaS or SaaS

As also seen in Figure 1 –contemporary infrastructure includes traditional IT infrastructure, which has more or less stagnated, but also includes modern technology like cloud and virtual environment which is growing rapidly with most organizations adopting this due to the reduction in overall investment and cost, faster deployment and the possibility to ramp down when it isn't required.

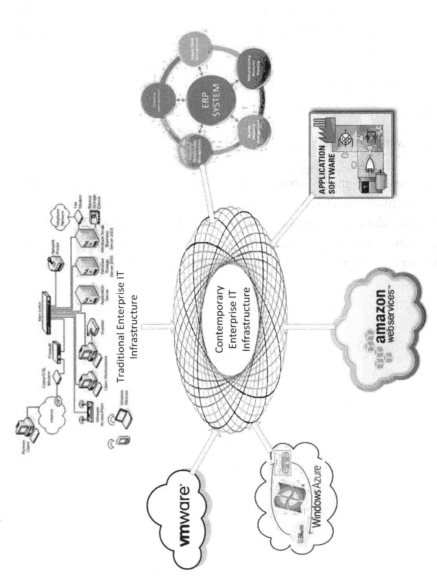

Figure 11: Contemporary Enterprise IT Infrastructure

In such an overly complex environment, what would be a sensible CMDB and how would you go about building it? We will attempt to answer this question with a suggested architecture.

2.8 Relevance of a CMDB in the contemporary IT world

Contemporary IT infrastructure in any enterprise usually includes a significant portion of virtual infrastructure and this is constantly increasing. Enterprises are also adopting public clouds and the rate of adoption will continue to grow.

Virtualization and the Cloud introduce several challenges towards building a traditional CMDB. The Virtual platform produces a new class of dynamic data that requires defining and capturing additional attributes for these CI's. In virtual environments, a new set of relationships between hosts, hypervisors, guests, virtual networks and virtual storage are created. Traditional CMDBs are not designed to handle these kinds of relationships. The lifecycle of the data is comparatively shorter as new information is created at a very rapid rate and the typical data update process and frequency for updates in traditional CMDB implementations are unable to handle this. When services are running in a public cloud, they cannot be discovered using standard discovery methods used to discover infrastructure within private datacenters and this poses significant data collection challenges to determine the relationship between the CI's. It feels like we are returning to the early days, where, when services were sourced externally, this ended up being a black box service as assets were not hosted or owned by organizations themselves and customers had no visibility or control over what went on at the backend.

Does that mean the CMDB has become irrelevant? If you have been imagining the CMDB as a central, sole and core database and a source of all of the information, then probably yes, it has become irrelevant. But in reality, the CMDB is not a central, sole or core database and it certainly is not the only source of information so the question itself becomes irrelevant. The relevance is also tied to the purpose. So the more appropriate question is whether the CMDB is relevant for its intended purpose? Or is the purpose itself now irrelevant? Let me draw an analogy – has traditional IT become irrelevant because of the cloud?

The CMDB as an important information provider will remain relevant, but the methods and technologies to build, discover, collate, federate, represent and operate the CMDB will constantly get adjusted with the operating environment.

In fact, the real issue is organizations try and engineer the CMDB to provide data that is probably not relevant in today's day and age, or shouldn't exist in the CMDB anyway, or is easily available from another data source. With the adoption of virtual servers, one big issue is that information that may theoretically have existed in the CMDB (i.e. relationships between CI's) gets created or changes at a very rapid rate. Hundreds of new guests can get provisioned in time periods much too short to allow for the traditional method of "Extract, Transform and Load" processes that feed information into the CMDB's and this method of data transfer for this class of CI's is no longer possible. The environment can change at a rate that existing CMDB's cannot keep up with. Something as simple as vMotion (where the management console of the virtual infrastructure in VMWare, a leading virtualization technology provider, moves virtual machines from one physical host to another to better utilize processing capacity, memory, etc.) events can create thousands of configuration changes in a few minutes; something that the typical CMDB architecture is simply not designed to keep up with. It is not practical to try and squeeze this into the old, rigid way of working. The movement of the guest hosts is applicable in a clustered environment. In this environment, virtual machine to cluster is meaningful to hold in the CMDB, but virtual machine to the physical host is overkill. It is additionally not advisable to even attempt to do this, as it not be possible to keep the information up to date and if you can't trust the data when you need to refer to it, what's the point of holding it? The internal workings of the virtual environment is "internal run time data" that is not governed by traditional change management process and does not really need to be loaded in CMDB. This is not only unwarranted but also unrealistic. Besides this VCOPs (the management console for VMWare's virtualization environment) is a MDR by itself. It holds all the information regarding the physical and virtual machines, their relationships, etc. and you do not need to replicate every piece of information from the MDR to the CMDB. CMDB ought to be at an abstraction level of individual MDRs.

The similar issue also exists in another area of infrastructure management and one that has been recognized and resolved several years ago. Almost all hardware vendors include capability or monitoring tools that will proactively monitor the health of their hardware devices, so that any issues can be picked up as quickly as possible or in some cases, even before they happen. However, one monitoring tool per technology type is difficult to manage. Additionally, there are many monitoring tools in the market that are designed to monitor cross platform devices (servers, network, storage), software, log files, processes and services, operating systems, etc. In any typical organization, monitoring is done using a combination of these tools. Anyone who is familiar with "event management" and monitoring, will be aware that these tools generate thousands of events and alerts every minute. Not all are "issues", these tools even generate informational events. Now imagine trying to view these events on each tools individual console – it would just not be practical. Also, each of these tools, monitoring each individual technology type, could throw up multiple events for a single issue. For example, if a switch in a data center were to become unavailable, all the servers that were connected to it would be unreachable, all the applications running on these servers would be unusable by end users and each individual component would generate an alert. This would cause each event being diagnosed and worked on individually, which would not be efficient use of resources. To overcome this issue, organizations deploy a "manager of mangers" – which acts as the overarching collation tool for events. It doesn't deal with all the noise, but only pre-defined event types and correlated events are represented to the end user, so that they can deal with the real issue at hand, rather than have to cut through all the noise in the lower level event management tools. The raw data is still available in the element monitoring tools for further detailed analysis. A similar approach is what is required for the CMDB – which should act as the "manager of managers" for

CI information, where selective information is forwarded from the MDR's, which hold detailed information for these CI's.

Emerging ITBM need and CMDB

Most organizations struggle with trying to measure and calculate if IT acts as a strategic differentiator to their business or a just a commodity item. Calculating the cost of IT services is easy if looked at holistically, but measuring the accurate cost for each discrete service can end up being very complex, since many of the underlying components are shared across many services. Some organizations treat IT as just another internal cost center, others separate IT as a separate business to provide services to other internal lines of businesses whilst IT can be the business for others, e.g. large IT service providers. In these cases, measuring the actual cost of the service becomes vitally important to efficiently and successfully manage it as a business.

In order to calculate the costs of providing services it is necessary to design and build a framework in which all costs can be recorded and allocated or apportioned to specific services, business units, locations, customers or other activities. Such 'Cost Models' can be developed to actually charge back to the business or as a 'show-back' show, for example, the cost of each service, the cost for each Customer or the cost for each location. Such cost models or financial management of IT services cannot be done if the underlying components, their relationships and understanding which IT services they support are not properly understood. What this means is that if a CMDB doesn't exist, you will not be able to do accurate financial or IT business management. You can of course take an approach to calculate the total cost of IT and just apportion it out to each business unit, but that would not correctly depict what each service is costing.

There has been a recent spate of several vendors that provide software which claim to help organizations understand and benchmark their IT Costs or to accurately know the cost per application and service and then show the business these detailed figures to be able to analyze the value and even automate the planning and forecasting for future budgets. This all sounds amazing! In fact when they actually do demonstrations to CIO's with fancy and colorful graphs and charts, they are completely blown away and wonder how they have survived for so long without this software. It is crucial for any organization to understand where they are spending their money and this magical software seems to be the one to not only tell them where they they their dollars are being consumed, but can go as far as telling them how much they will need to spend in the future!

Unfortunately, what every ITBM software vendor fails to tell the CIO is that without the underlying data, the software will not be able to deliver to any of its claims. The software needs to be fed detailed information of the components that make up each of the services, how they are all related to each other and how much of it is consumed by which business unit. Yes, we do agree that some of the ITBM applications probably provide some excellent dashboard capability with pre-built cost models that can be configured to consume data from the ITSM tools and then provide pretty graphs, charts, reports and different views of the data, but at its bare bones, the tool is no good without accurate and complete data being fed into it from the CMDB. So without a CMDB, which is the primary provider of data for financial management, no ITBM software will be able to function. Successfully implementing a CMDB can constitute almost 80% of an ITBM project with the other 20% being taking the data, creating the cost models, calculating the costs and displaying them in the required view.

2.9   Relevance of a CMDB for SIAM

SIAM (Service Integration and Management) has been consistently named as a top IT and Business service related challenge time and again in various reports and studies. One reason for SIAM's rise in importance is that organizations are heterogeneous at their core, consuming best of breed services from vendors they painstakingly select and manage. In simple terms Service integration and management (SIAM) is an approach to managing multiple suppliers of information technology services and integrating them to deliver a unified business-facing IT organization. The "Service Management" part here is the management of the service life cycle right from strategy to transition to operation to improvement whereas the "Service Integration" part is the 'binding together' of multiple service providers and streamlining their multiple processes and tools to deliver a cohesive service working as a single unit. Bringing together multiple suppliers, each with their own style of working, processes, tools etc. and molding them into one cohesive service is not a walk in the park. The services and the criticality of a supplier in the service value chain decides the accountabilities and the roles. Since very clear accountabilities between different suppliers is difficult to achieve, especially in today's dynamic, complex and often-times cloud based IT environment, this becomes one of the major challenges while implementing SIAM.

The CMDB plays a critical part in successfully integrating and managing services provided by discrete suppliers and managing them as a whole. If the components within the service delivery chain are not clearly understood, if who is responsible for them when things go wrong is not known and how they all relate to each other is a mystery, then the supplier eco system cannot be managed, i.e. if the CMDB is not implemented, the ambition of adopting a SIAM model would not be possible. This in fact needs to be extended even further to support SAIM. While the CMDB provide a route map for service delivery components (CI's) and their interrelationships, to understand the impact of these services on business requires that this mapping is extended to the service and process layers. This helps cover additional attributes to support the SIAM organization (e.g. the SLA, the criticality, the vendor supporting the CI, their support hours, etc.). These service maps form a critical component for implementation especially if the SIAM function is being provided by an external supplier, as they may not have adequate visibility or the understanding of the complexities and inter-dependencies of the prevalent environment. We have discussed service maps in more detail further in this book.

2.10 *Changing needs with change in technology*

Technology is constantly evolving and it is happening at a very rapid pace. There is a constant focus on trying to get things done faster, quicker and cheaper. As the technical landscape changes, our needs from the CMDB change too. For some of these advances, we want more information, for others we are looking for less. In a lot of cases, even if we do want information to be held in the CMDB, it becomes difficult and sometime impossible to be able to get that data; for example – with the virtual servers moving to different hosts as described above.

Evolution of technology brought into virtualization, which helped to reduce complexity in the environment by reducing the number of physical hosts. Several instance of servers can be hosted on a single physical host. This reduced the overall cost, rack space requirement, energy and resource cost. However, it brought its own sets of challenges. It still involves investing in servers and software and maintaining that infrastructure. Its greatest benefit is reducing the cost of that infrastructure for companies by maximizing the usage of the physical resources.

While virtualization may be used to provide cloud computing (private and public clouds), they are actually different. Cloud computing may look like virtualization, because it appears that your application is running on a virtual server, and they are similar in that fashion. However, cloud computing can be better described as a service where virtualization is part of the physical infrastructure. Private clouds are where this infrastructure is deployed within your own (or leased) data centers, whereas, the public could is where this is procured from a 3rd party and consumed over the internet without the need to having this implemented within your data centers.

Each set of technology and advancement introduced its own set of challenges with regards to holding information in the CMDB.

Virtualization and CMDB

Due to the constantly changing data within the virtual environments, replicating the information in the CMDB is no long an option. The better approach to handle situations like this would be to 'reference' the information in the management console of the virtualization technology, so that it may be represented and visible in the CMDB, while not actually being physically replicated in there. The virtualization management console becomes the MDR for the entire virtual estate. It also then has the added advantage of always presenting the user with the most accurate information, which is one of the basic and fundamental requirements from a CMDB (i.e. accuracy).

The information held in the CMDB should be limited to the physical hosts, whereas the virtual guests hosted instead being retained within the management console of the virtualization technology and being referenced and queried in real time from the CMDB when required.

The Cloud and the CMDB

With the constant pressure to provide more for less with shrinking budgets, cloud computing, software as a service, in fact, everything as a service is here to stay and phenomenally grow. Almost all organizations, both big and small are moving towards adopting the cloud to fulfil more and more of their IT computing needs. There are of course several advantages of using the cloud in overall investment and cost, faster deployment and the possibility to ramp down when it isn't required, this however also brings in the disadvantage of having control or even visibility on the back end infrastructure. Is this really a disadvantage? Do we even really care what sits behind the service that we consume on the cloud as long as we have an SLA for availability of the service?

With the adaption of the cloud in an organization, the CMDB needs to be adapted to accommodate this. The service that is being consumed in the cloud is held as a 'service' CI, with only the relevant service attributes rather than 'server' attributes, which would have been the case if it was a server installed within the organizations data center. An example of a few typical attributes that you would hold for a 'service' CI are:

Attribute	Description
Service ID	Index number for the service
Service Class	Business/enabling IT/etc.
Service Category	Organizes services according to type and target audiences
Service Name	Identifies name of the infrastructure services being provided
Service Status	Identifies status as one of the following: • Proposed – service under development and not yet live • Live – service offered in production • Archived – service no longer offered
Description	Offers a brief description of the service in customer (nontechnical) terms
Key Service Deliverables	Describes features and functions of the service available to any user who receives the service as per SLA
Business Owner	Identifies a business unit point of contact. This is usually from the unit that sponsor or pay for the service
IT Owner	Identifies the IT support group lead in case of a service outage or performance degradation
Customer (Dept./Business Unit)	Identifies which business units/departments are eligible to receive the service
User Requirements	Indicates pre-requisites that a user should have in order to successfully receive the service

Attribute	Description
Assurance	Utility and warranty assurance
Service Level - Availability	Agreed uptime of the service based on SLA
Service Hours	Describes service availability hours e.g. 24X7
Support Hours	Describes service support hours in case of outage or break fix
Support SLA	Agreed response & resolution/fulfillment time
Service Price	Indicates any per user, department or business unit costs associated with the standard service deliverables
Criticality	Associated business criticality of the service and its availability in for the DR (disaster recovery) environment
User Types	Is this an internal/external facing service
Managed or Supported By	The IT support team that manages the service. This would typically be the team that has control of the cloud service management console.

The level of abstraction held in the CMDB is slowly going higher and higher as we adopt new technology and as it gets cheaper. A field replaceable unit (FRU) is a part that can be quickly and easily be replaced by a user or technician without having to send the entire system to a repair facility. FRUs allow the technician to not have in-depth knowledge to repair a component, but instead to just replace the faulty part. The granularity of the FRUs are usually dictated by the cost. If a part is cheap and easily available, it rarely is worth training resources on how to repair it, spending the time, effort and money on bringing units back to a facility to repair, etc. It may be easier to just replace the part. When consuming infrastructure as a service in the cloud, the entire server effectively becomes an 'FRU'. If it stops functioning, it fails over to another server to provide the service. So as far as the organization consuming the service on the cloud – the server is the lowest level and is held as a service rather than a server with detailed components.

IOT and CMDB

Internet of Things (IOT) is rapidly evolving and is an innovation area across many IT departments. The technology is being considered for a lot of different innovative solutions. In the context of IOT, the "things" communicate and collaborate with each other. The 'thing" in "Internet of Things" could be just about anything – goods, objects, machines, appliances, buildings, vehicles, animals, people (yes, you will also merely be a data point in an IOT world), plant, basically anything you can name. At the core of IOT is each thing having a unique ID on the Internet (can be achieved with IP V6 addressing scheme), sensing capabilities and communicating capabilities. With these capabilities, you can monitor things, manage things and control things. Although, the uptake has been most visible in the home or consumer technology space with all sorts of devices that can now be controlled over the internet and via mobile apps, etc. You see this from fridges to home heating systems, etc. Several businesses have also been looking to IoT to explore what business issues can be resolved using the technology. Retail and logistics are expected to have a major impact with this enabling technology. Refrigerated transportation organizations looking to monitor, control and adjust the temperature in their trucks as goods are transported, or leveraging IoT in supply chain optimization with the modularization of production lines.

The IoT is not just a technology to be used for consumer products, neither is it an answer to advancement in the industrial sector or only a solution to some business issued. At its heart, it is about using increased connectivity to exchange and share data, then make decisions based on this information. The decision making can of course be automated based on predefined rules. The extent of the inroads that IoT is making into IT means that support teams need to understand what impact this has on the services they provide, how they provide support services and be ready to respond.

Understanding the impact of CI's on other CI's plays a key role in easing the complexity burden created by the IoT. When the IOT is used in an enterprise (e.g. manufacturing, supply chain, etc.), the CMDB would enable you to visualize and understand the different supporting components relate to one another. The connected devices that will interact with the network translate into more CI's that can be adversely impacted by a change. A robust change management process would be vital to dealing with this increased complexity. This frees support and IT workers to see how one change will impact other systems and avoid making a decision that unexpectedly causes problems. The surge of items connecting to the network and the complexity of the interdependency between networked devices makes increased visibility essential. In the IOT world, a "thing" will not only provide some type of service but also consume services as well. In this context, everything becomes a CI. Today, in the infancy of the IOT world, we have a thing surrounded by less than ten things (appliances, thermostat, car, door etc.), but it is predicted that in a decade or so, the count will go to hundreds or even thousands. In today's enterprise IT, the ratio of a service provider things to service consumer things is very high and within a manageable number of service provider things, so the need to manage service provider things makes the CMDB relevant. Due to so many devices reliant on the service, its criticality increases, but this would be true of any business or mission critical service. However, in the IOT world envisioned in the future, even in enterprise IT, with the adoption of IOT, the numbers of endpoints or devices consuming services grows much larger and the ratio will be almost 1:1 – which means every service provider will be a service consumer also, at which point, holding of this in the CMDB would not be possible. In fact, a CMDB would not be required either because things will be self-managed, self-learning as well as self-healing.

2.10.1 Typical CMDB Architecture

The architecture in Figure 12 is a pragmatic approach to manage heterogeneous data sources and building and maintaining the CMDB in today's contemporary IT environment.

A typical CMDB (centralized view within the ITSM system) will usually source data from multiple disparate sources:

1. Directly receive data from the discovery tools during the build phase and only after a qualified change has been executed in the operation phase.

2. Data from the reconciliation engine which combines, cleans, transforms and provides consolidated data from multiple discovery tools or data sources; this is applicable both during the initial build stage as well as during the operation phase)

3. It is impossible to collect all the data required in a CMDB via automated discovery tools. To have a meaningful CMDB that provides value, it will have to be overlay with manual data. This may also be the method to provide all information for certain CI's. The manual data – structured or unstructured will be populated in the CMDB, both during the initial build as well as during the operation phase

4. Federated data from multiple MDRs – Data is referenced only. Data view during operation phase

The burden of data accuracy is on the CMDB itself for data that is sourced from sources 1-3 above. For the data that is federated, the burden of accuracy is on MDRs as it is held and maintained there with no control from the CMDB. The issue is actually simplified because a larger problem of completeness and accuracy is sliced in to multiple smaller problems and each slice is handed over to a different party to tackle.

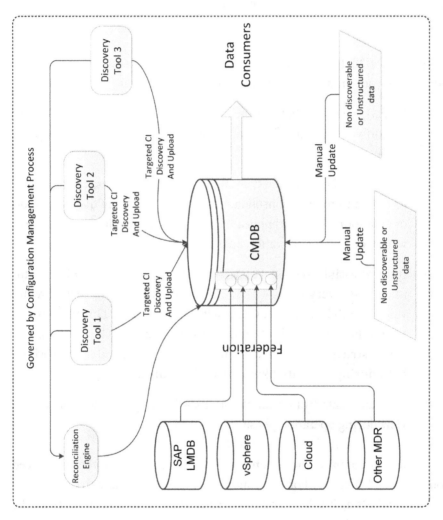

Figure 12: typical CMDB Architecture for contemporary IT Infrastructure

2.11 ITSM and CMDB

By the term ITSM, in this section, we are referring to the tool for IT support services used for core support processes like incident management, change management, problem management, request management etc. The CMDB is an integral part of this tool, although, the CMDB can quite easily be built outside of the ITSM tool just like the MDR.

There are however multiple advantages of building the CMDB within ITSM tool

1. Easy to use – Biggest consumers of CMDB data are change management, incident management and problem management. These processes run in the ITSM tool and the data in the CMDB is shareable within the same system and is just a click away

2. Cost advantage – you do not need to buy any additional tool or the infrastructure to host it

3. Faster to implement – you receive a predefined data model and prebuilt functionality for integration of the CMDB with other processes within the ITSM tool

4. Easy to implement control processes and access controls

5. Easy integrations due to adapters provided by vendors or support for standard integration protocols

The only disadvantage is that all ITSM tools provide the CMDB on a relational database that is not really designed for this purpose or able to handle the requirements of the contemporary IT environment. In support of this argument, we want to cite the example of BMC ADDM (Application Discovery and Dependency Manager, previously called Tideway), which is sold as a discovery tool, but it is in fact a wonderful standalone CMDB and it is not in a relational database.

Another disadvantage with most of the ITSM tools that boast of their CMDBs is that they mix the asset DB and CMDB. As stated in section 2.6.1, the asset

DB is a simpler database and complex process, while the CMDB is a complex database and a simpler process. It is easier to manage one complexity at a time and by combining both, you would find you multiply the complexity, making it far more difficult to both implement and maintain.

2.12 A case for CMDB in Graph Database

RDBMSs cannot model or store data and its relationships without complexity, and performance degrades with the number and levels of data relationships and data size. What's more, adding new types of data and data relationships requires schema redesign that increases time to market. For these reasons, RDBMSs are inappropriate when data relationships are valuable in real time. Having discussed the lacunae of a relational DB, we want to present a case for suitability of a Graph Database for building the CMDB.

Graphs are used to model many types of relations and processes in almost all genres in life including physical, biological, social and information systems. Especially in information systems, graphs are used to represent networks of communication, data organization, the flow of data or any other kind of information. A well understood example is a website graph representing the link structure of a website where the vertices represent web pages and directed edges represent links from one page to another. If you are storing the information in tabular form and viewing the information in graphical form then you need to add an additional layer of processing to create the views. Why not store the information directly in the form of a graph and have a native view? That is what a graph database can do.

The importance and the need for visualization in a CMDB are very well understood. It improves the usability of the CMDB significantly. CMDB tools now add a visualization layer, but in many cases, charge extra for the feature. A graph database makes it simple and saves potential costs.

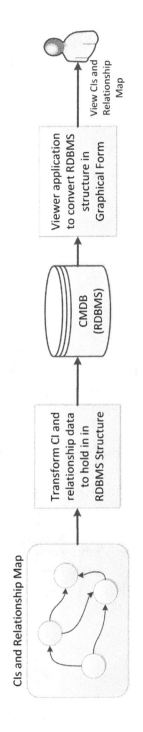

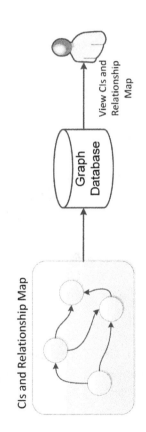

Figure 13: Simplicity with Graph Database

Graph database is a NOSQL (Not Only SQL) database, but not all NOSQL databases are graph databases. NOSQL is a very wide category for a group of persistence solutions which don't follow the relational data model, and who don't use SQL as the query language.

NOSQL databases can be categorized according to their data model into the following four categories:

- Key value stores

- BigTable implementations

- Document stores

- Graph databases

A graph database is a database that uses a graph structure with nodes, edges and properties to represent and store information. We always want to see the CI and their relationships in graphical form and this is exactly how it is natively stored in a graph database. Therefore a graph databases, by design, are the best medium to build a CMDB on.

For the purpose of illustration, depicted below is the view of a CI in a graph database. This is a straight forward view of discovery via Nmap ("Network Mapper" is a free and open source (license) utility for network discovery) and Neo4 – a graph database

Additionally, Graph databases are designed in a more event driven fashion and are massively scalable by design which can be leveraged to address the high rate of change of CI data/attributes/relationships that are dynamic in next gen IT operations.

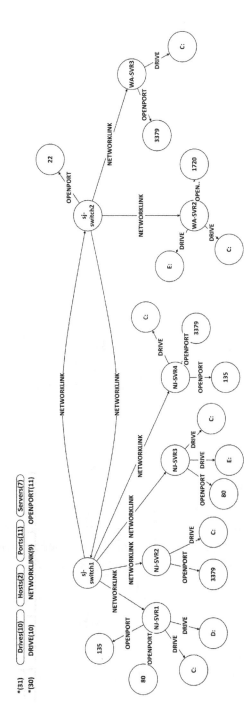

Figure 14: CMDB view in graph database

3 BUILDING CMDB

CMDB as envisioned by most of managers is usually beyond the means of most organizations. For those who can afford it, it is seldom the best use of funds. So embark upon a CMDB project only after you have qualified the need of a CMDB from both the ROI and ROCE perspectives. Most of your needs will likely be fulfilled by a good asset management and distributed MDR's. For example, in today's IT environments, the two most critical centrally managed environments are ERP and virtual infrastructure and both can be managed with its own MDR support. Your ERP system will have its own CMDB (like SAP LMDB) and your virtual infrastructure will have a virtual center DB as a comprehensive MDR. In our opinion, the need of asset management is stronger than the need of a CMDB. However, there are cost justifications for building and maintaining a good CMDB. A deep CMDB for limited number of business critical applications should make a good business case. Nevertheless, you may need to serve a larger purpose and need to build a CMDB, so let's look at the next steps.

The very first principle of building the CMDB is to design top down and implement bottom up. To successfully design and build the CMDB you would follow a four step approach. This is typical for any tool deployment:

1. Plan

2. Architect

3. Design

4. Build

You must have answers to several key questions for a successful build. Some of these questions are listed below; we also provide some the guidance and views around several of these questions.

1. How should the data model be aligned with the overall enterprise IT (Architect phase)?

2. What are the taxonomy standards to be followed (Design Phase)

3. What is the granularity of CI's that you need to hold in the CMDB (Design Phase)?

4. What are the structural components and CIs (Planning)?

5. What is the physical and function characteristics of CIs (Design)?

6. What are the CI classes and attributes (Design) that you need to have populated in the CMDB based on your requirements?

7. What type of relationship classes and attributes (Design) do you need to hold?

8. How do you need to classification and categorize (Design) other tickets and CI's?

9. What naming conventions (Design) need to be followed?

10. What is your data collection strategy (Planning)?

11. What are your different data sources (Build)?

12. What is your strategy for discovery of CI's and which tools are to be used (Planning)?

13. How is data going to be collected and eventually kept up to date (Build)?

14. What data validation rules are to be followed (Build)?

15. How is data validation going to be performed (Plan/Build)?

16. How will data correction be performed (Plan/Build)?

17. What methods and criteria will you use to measure the accuracy and relevance of the CMDB (Design)?

3.1 Plan

When you are planning to build an information system like a CMDB, you must first develop a vision and a strategy. A vision is the future looking end state statement, while the strategy is a statement of how you will achieve the vision. We would like to add one more very important question – how will you sustain it? In other words, just a roadmap or strategy on how you will attain it is not good enough you're your strategy must include a plan on how you will sustain the relevance, accuracy, completeness and purpose of the CMDB.

The planning stage when designing and building a CMDB is much more comprehensive than most people think. It is not the same as implementing another tool that collects and holds data. Apart from planning on how the CMDB is to be designed, implemented, integrated and populated, it is equally important to ensure that planning for the operate phase is also taken into account with a very clear understanding of how the data that is stored in the CMDB will be kept up to date. Of course, the methods and procedures for keeping up to date the data that is referenced from MDR's will remain with the data owners of the MDR. The scope of the typical planning stage for a CMDB project is depicted in Figure 15 below:

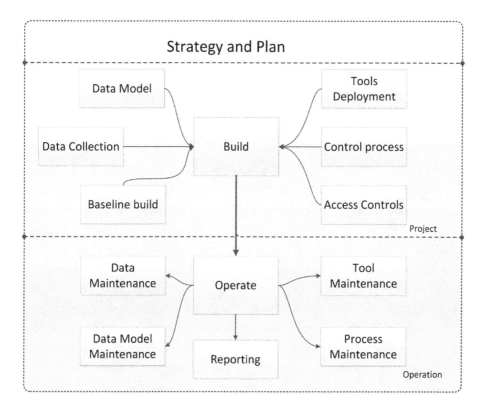

Figure 15: Scope of planning

Develop CMDB Vision and CMDB Strategy

To develop a CMDB strategy, first start by gathering requirements and wish list from all stakeholders, who are eventually the teams that will become users of the CMDB, such as the data center team, the disaster recovery (DR) Team, database teams, network teams, storage teams, application teams, service delivery managers, etc. These groups will eventually be the consumers of the data in the CMDB and therefore the customers of the CMDB service provider. They will also become data providers in several situations, so it is a good idea to already start setting the expectation that for all the requirements to hold certain information, it is quite likely that they will have to play a part in providing the information for it too.

Understand existing tool landscape

If you look at any organization, you will find that they have procured a whole plethora of tools over time, many of which end up becoming shelf ware. Decisions to buy tools are driven by individual groups to solve a specific issue or to manage a specific technology area, very rarely based on a Lots of these different tools will also end up having some duplicate functionality. Vendors also bundle tools with other software they sell. Organizations end up with lots and lots of different tools, several of which are bought based on hype from software vendors and no clear tools strategy. It is important to understand the existing tools landscape when scoping the CMDB project and understanding different possible data sources, it also provides the perfect opportunity to also plan out a tools rationalization strategy and highlight tools that are not used, can be decommissioned or tools that provide duplicate functionality.

Evaluate & identify the tool set for CMDB and configuration management

Once you have a rock solid understanding of what you need to achieve with the CMDB, what your data sources are going to be, what information you will hold and how it will be consumed, selection of the CMDB tool is not hard, although it is an important decision. Most ITSM tools also include a CMDB and this is the most commonly adopted approach. Most organizations build their CMDB within the ITSM tool itself. This has several advantages, including pre-built availability of the data in the CMDB for the other ITSM processes it supports by virtue of existing in the same toolset. Depending on your requirements, including considerations of integrations with the different data sources or with multiple MDR's, the CMDB within the ITSM toolset will more than likely serve your purpose. Now, if you have not selected your ITSM tool as yet, that is a much larger question and an extremely critical one. A wrong decision and you could have to live it with for a long time. The requirements for the CMDB should feed into the considerations, plan and vision for the ITSM tool, if the CMDB is to be held in there.

Depending on your requirements, you may even consider holding the CMDB outside of the ITSM tool, some may even consider building this within the discovery tool. Strange as the approach of building the CMDB in the discovery tool may sound, we had mentioned BMC ADDM as a possible candidate for this in section 2.11, which could meet the requirements of a CMDB, of course that would depend entirely on your requirements.

Develop Roadmap

A roadmap is a plan that with short and long term goals to achieve the vision and strategy for the CMDB utilizing technology solutions to help meet those goals. In order to create the CMDB roadmap, certain set of knowledge and skills will be required. This means that some of the participants must know the technology that the CMDB will be built on, its capabilities, integration methods it supports, time it would take to build functionality in the tool, it's out of the box data model, etc. Additional tribal organizational knowledge would also be required with a fair understanding of current data availability in the organization to be able to populate the CMDB, as all of these will impact the stages and milestones in the roadmap.

The CMDB cannot all be populated at the same time and not all data sources will or should be integrated at the same time. Several data sources will have dependency on other data already being available so that it can be overlaid on top of it. To refer to a previous analogy – you first have to have the geographical maps before you can overlay the restaurants within a geographical area. Developing a roadmap will also serve three other critical criteria for success:

1. Verify and get agreement on the set of requirements; this will also serve another purpose of documenting the scope and boundaries for the build phase, so that the project start and end can be defined.

2. Ensure agreement on the technologies and data sources required to satisfy those needs;

3. Provide a framework with measureable milestone to help plan and build the CMDB

The CMDB roadmap must clearly articulate:

1. Identify the "product/tool" that will be used for the CMDB

2. Identify the data sources for each of the CI classes to be available in the CMDB (based on the requirements gathered)

3. Identify the methods that the sources will provide data to the CMDB:

    a. Will it be *extracted, transformed*, and *loaded*? Will that via an integration, FTP file exchange, etc.?

    b. Will it be referenced (e.g. to an MDR)?

4. Identify which discovery tools also need to be implemented to feed the CMDB.

5. Identify the external systems that the CMDB needs to feed data to (if any) and what integrations are required for that

Last, but not the least, the roadmap should provide the sequence in which these milestones will be achieved and what data is expected to be available in the CMDB at each stage. This will also help to plan the follow on tasks of enriching the data with additional manual inputs, for which the effort required should not be under estimated, especially since the input will be required from multiple teams in different parts of the IT organization.

Once the roadmap has been created, you must verify if the roadmap can support that vision and its goals.

Assess the need for enhancement of the supporting process

Most organizations approach a CMDB project is a technology implementation project. In large parts it is a technical deployment as a "database" is being built that will hold all this valuable information and it will be integrated with several external systems, etc. The project becomes a tool project without a lot of focus on the supporting processes needed to manage the data into the CMDB. The CMDB will not remain accurate for very long or provide any real value if there aren't controls in place to ensure effective updates to the CMDB. We have discussed the overall arching configuration management process in chapter 7.1 of this book.

Refer to Figure 15 above, which clearly shows the activities in both the build and operate phase. E.g. data maintenance during the operate phase. Each of these activities require a formal, defined, agreed process with clear roles and responsibilities. The easiest way to do a gap analysis for enhancement of support processes is to identify what processes already exist that need to be revised or which ones need to be defined from scratch.

Define the CMDB Scope

Building a complete CMDB is a long journey. In fact, you could argue that it will never be entirely complete. There will always be additions to it and it will evolve as your IT landscape changes. At the same time, to ensure that your efforts can be measured and that it meets the expectations, you should identify the short and long terms scope, including what CI classes you will hold, what attributes are to be available in both the short and long term (how wide and how deep). It should also describe where data is to be consumed from and how the CMDB is to be populated in each stage, i.e. it is manually imported initially and then automated at a later stage, is it federated and referenced, etc. Once both the long and short term scope has been agreed, it is time to develop a project plan that can be funded, resourced and executed.

Prepare Project Plan

A detailed and executable project plan must be developed, that clearly identifies dependencies, resources and measurable milestones. Depending on your environment, the plan may also include the architecture design and implementation of discovery tools. It will certainly include tasks for implementing the CMDB, building a baseline, integrating it with your data sources, testing by use cases of the consumption of the data in the CMDB by the ITSM processes and eventually training both data owners and users on how to navigate, search, use and maintain the data in the CMDB.

Review and Agree on Project Plan

At the end of the planning, you must have a clear answer to one of the most important questions - what data do you need to hold as well as reference in the CMDB. This is not an easy answer, especially because every stakeholder has his own purpose and use of the CMDB. Someone may want to use it as an asset database, someone else would want to consume all their data needs from a centralized consolidated information system, someone else may want to use it as a data provider for event management correlation, while someone will want to use as the source data for billing or chargeback to other parts of the organization.

These may all be valid and justified uses, but start with the most basic and common uses and try to fulfill those first and then expand at a later stage. Trying to satisfy a very small subset of requirements will not be the best way to approach this, additionally there is a logical sequence to building the CMDB – remember, "the very first principle of building the CMDB is to design top down and implement bottom up". Attempting to meet every purpose or everyone's wish list will jeopardize the project. The most important guideline for what type of data should be available in the CMDB is look at this the other way around and instead consider what type of data should not be held in the CMDB and that is – *any data elements that are not under change control OR any data elements for which you cannot implement an update process; should not be kept in the CMDB.* The very purpose of the CMDB is to provide reliable and accurate information. If you do not maintain the integrity of the data by change control or the accuracy by timely update processes, then the basic purpose of the CMDB will be defeated. This qualification paradigm will challenge the tendency to hold the following data elements:

1. The data regarding development environments – the CMDB is focused on the CIs and relationships of service producing systems and their impact on a service. You maintain the integrity of production environments. It is not viable to maintain the integrity of development environments as this is constantly changing by its very nature

2. Asset data such as the asset status and financial attributes – the financial property of a CI has no impact on the service it produces or supports

3. Desktop and laptop records – desktops and laptops are service consuming end points and not a service producing systems. In our view, desktops and laptops should be held in an asset database, but not held as CIs.

4. Several data elements or attributes related to the virtual environments. For example a virtual machine's host name and IP may be the right data elements for the CMDB but the physical to logical relationship, that is constantly changing will be overkill in the CMDB

5. Several data elements related to cloud computing, for example a virtual machine that is hosted in the cloud is more likely a managed object rather than a CI. You do not manage that VM as it is procured as a service, but only monitor its state - whether it is running or has shut down.

Some of the data elements that are not under change control but are useful to support the change management process are the roles associated with CIs. Every CI will have a business owner and a technical owner, usually stored as an attribute "owned by" and "managed by" fields in the CMDB. These values are used for the approval processes when change requests are raised for that CI. These are not under change control but will require a process to ensure that the data is maintained.

When you have completed your plan, you should also have clear answers to questions like:

1. Operational RACI (responsibility, accountability, consulted, informed matrix)

2. Key performance indicators (KPI) and reporting requirements

3. Operational team size required

3.2 Architecture

The Architecture defines the various parts of the CMDB that will be integrated and eventually work together to provide an end to end usable service. The architecture will reflect the vision of your CMDB. We can all appreciate how important it is to establish an architecture that is future proof and protect the investment in the CMDB. Typical information that is included in an architecture for a CMDB are:

1. Physical and logical structure of the CMDB

2. How the data elements are organized

3. What are the individual data sources

4. How they are connected or integrated

5. Data flow and controls

6. Data model at the top level

7. Compliance with enterprise architecture standards

Section 2.10 provides an example of the architecture for a CMDB.

3.3 Design

The design takes the architecture blue print and details it out to create detailed design specifications. The first and the most important part to design is the data model. This has been discussed in section 3.3.2.

Another important part is the design of the tool to be used for the CMDB or to support it, like discovery tools. You will not actually design the tool as this is more than likely to be a commercial off the shelf product, but you will need to design the integrations between these tools and the federation of your data sources. There are three broad categories of tools that you would need

1. ITSM tool – as the core CMDB will be an integral part of the ITSM tool. The ITSM tool will also help you to build control processes

2. Discovery tools – you will more than likely have more than one tool in this category

3. Other utility tools depending on your architecture such as a reconciliation engine, ETL, e-bonding or broker, etc.

3.3.1 Data access control

Access to the CMDB also needs to be controlled. Three levels of access are generally required – to view a CI record, modify a CI record and add a new

CI record. The granularity of access provided would depend upon the process and policies that you establish for data maintenance.

View access could be unrestricted within the boundary of service delivery and service support staff. Within view access, you can define restrictions for certain fields to limit the viewing of this data to only certain resources or teams.

Modify access is typically controlled and not provided to everybody. Data modification is usually done by automated methods, example discovery tools, but since all data cannot be discovered, this is usually enriched by additional manual methods as well. For manual updating of records, there could be a centralized role that can update a CI record only if certain conditions are met. (A RFC was implemented successfully for example). Alternatively, class based update rights can be granted – for example the network management team member could update CI records for the network class. The difficulty in this method is designing the update rights for relationship across two different classes of Cis.

Access for CI creation is normally even more strictly controlled. CI's can theoretically be created by systems or humans. The majority of the CI's in the CMDB will be created by automated means like discovery tools or external systems like asset databases. These tools are granted the rights to create CI's directly, but in most cases, this will also be controlled and only done after reconciliation and verification of the data. In several cases, CI's will need to be created by humans too, for which the appropriate access needs to be provided. An example would be to create "service" class CI's which would not be discoverable. These are us typically services with business friendly names and are a combination of supporting application CI's.

Data views

Storing the data within the CMDB is an important aspect however displaying the data for easy navigation and usability is another point to consider.

Usability and the ability to get to the required information quickly and easily is an important criteria. If you have the data, but can't access it easily, it may not be used as much as you would like. For example, if a server administrator needs to view the host name, IP address and a few other important attributes - on one screen. The IP address could be a CI class by itself, where the IP address of a server would be an instance of that class, with a relationship to the server. This is a common scenario and we have come across this in several implementations. The data in this case would actually be stored in two different tables – as they are both separate CI's (the server and the IP address). From a data management perspective, it is probably easier to define and manage the IP address as a separate class, with a clearly defined data owner who has the responsibility to ensure it is maintained (the network support team). However, the users need is to display the server and its IP address on the same screen, i.e. as an attribute. These use cases must be considered and catered for whilst defining the data model. The requirements for usability and ensuring the required data views are incorporated in the functional design should be given equal importance.

3.3.2 Data Model

The data model defines how the data is stored in the database. The data model primarily determines the structure of the data. The processes that utilize the data, generate transaction data of their own. The transaction data generated will only be useful if it is structured and how you structure it is decided by the data model.

Badly designed data will have a direct impact on effectiveness of the process. A tool will always work with bad configuration data, but the process consuming this data will not be effective. We have come across all sorts of ITSM and CMDB implementations and the primary issues in most of these tool implementations are caused by poor or lack of any taxonomy standards. For a CMDB to record and manage data efficiently, the data model plays a very important role. The data model houses the place-holders for various types of CIs, their relationships and their attributes. Think of this as a chest of drawers, where each drawer holds a different type of clothing – socks in one, t-shirts in another, etc. Usually the service management tools provide a wide variety of options to pick and choose the best suited CI structure to fit the needs of the organization based on their IT Infrastructure. This ability to pick, choose and configured is provided because the vendors of these tools need to cater to the needs of IT organizations in various different industries and sectors. At the time of implementing a CMDB, the IT organization is required to narrow down the usage of CI classes and their attributes, as appropriate to their IT infrastructure.

ITIL versions have moved from a systems centric view (i.e. a *server* is unavailable) to a 'service' centric view (i.e. the *online trading service* is unavailable). This shift however also has an impact on the CMDB and its data model. The lower infrastructure components are easier to identify as they are physical components that can be touched, felt, so are easily recognizable (a server, disk, network devices, etc.) and can also be discovered. Once we move higher up the chain, away from the physical and to the CI's that are more abstract in nature, for example a 'service', it can get a lot more difficult. Most organizations even struggle to define what a service is, let alone actually be able to capture a list of their services. If you were to ask 10 people in a room, what in their view a service was, you will end up with about 13 different views, because 3 people will change their mind by the time you have asked everyone the question. This may be a bit of an exaggeration, but you get my message. Applications are also mixed up with services. The data model design, including classes, sub classes and its attributes must be clearly agreed prior to building the CMDB, including agreeing on what actually will go into each of these classes. List out the 'services' that your organization provides and agree which classes they will populate. This will also test your CMDB data model design.

In our experience, whenever we have seen implementations of CMDB's that delivered little value, insufficient importance was given to the design and planning of the data model. The ITSM tool does provide a data model, but it is designed with a view of fitting almost any organization, that its scope and set of classes is extremely large. Many of which may not be relevant to your organization. So organizations mostly end up using a much larger set of CI classes, which scatters the data over a greater number of classes of CIs than required for effective recording and management of the data. Listed below are some of the main disadvantages of an unplanned data model:

a. Substantial inconvenience in the ability to search for a CI due to the overload of visible options and drop down menus to navigate through and data being split in different tables, leading to looking each one up separately

b. Complex data mapping in the background, leading to an operational discomfort of complicated manual work/reconciliation rules required for updating the CMDB data

3.3.3 Taxonomy

'Taxonomy' is a system for naming and organizing things into groups that share similar characteristics. The terms taxonomy, cataloging, categorization and classification are often confused and used interchangeably. These are all ways of organizing information into categories.

Taxonomy is the organization of a particular set of information for a particular purpose. When implementing an ITSM tool, it helps to organize service management data for analysis, process improvement, KPI measurement as well as supporting other processes outside the ITSM tool.

Taxonomy is one of the methods available to efficiently manage the overload of information that we now face. While several tools may help to generate, retrieve, provide and measure information, each tool holds and categorizes data differently and its standards provide different benefits, but are rarely designed with a taxonomy taking a holistic view of the multiple tools working in synergy.

It is often necessary to accommodate the needs of multiple user groups, or, at a minimum, the different information seeking behaviors of people in a single user group. Therefore it is not necessary that the taxonomy applications (what the user sees) must conform to the same rules as the underlying taxonomy structure (how the data is stored on the system).

Data model Standard

The Common Information Model (CIM), standardized by DMTF (Distributed Management Task Force) is the industry standard data model that was designed for this purpose. It forms the foundation of almost every CMDB provided within commercial off the shelf ITSM tools. When you buy an ITSM tool, you also buy the predefined data model for the CMDB as decided by the ITSM tool vendor. Of course, they would have derived the guidance from the CIM, however, the vendor will also define additional CI classes and attributes, which will usually be built to sync with other products that they also sell, like discovery tools. You can add additional classes and attributes, but you should be very careful in doing so. You may break the predesigned field mapping used for integrating discovery tools with the CMDB.

What we have seen is that almost all CMDB data models provided by the different vendors, are overdesigned – in that it provides a very large number of classes and attributes/fields – many more that you would have required. In these cases, more is not necessarily good. It makes it more complex than is necessary and you will not use all the attributes and seek to hide several fields. Nevertheless, at the same time we have always come across the need for additional attributes and field. You should first explore relabeling an existing field which you aren't using, rather than creating a new field. However, also be careful with the relabeling, as this may require remapping of the field to the discovery tool, otherwise you will end up with data being stored and populated in the incorrect fields.

It is important to take usability considerations into account when defining CI classes in the data model. Classes are usually defined based on generic technology, but not all the time. It is common practice to define product based classes as well. "Network device", or "network gear" and "end user devices" are examples of generic technology based classes. However, when it comes to things like middleware or even virtualization technology, you will find product name based classes. The reason behind this is the traditional organization structure, where CMDB users are grouped according to the product name and/or technology class. Logically, middleware products can be placed into 6 generic categories namely - Message Oriented Middleware, Object Middleware, RPC Middleware, Database Middleware, Transaction Middleware and Portal/Web server. In this way, we would need only seven tables (One Middleware class and six sub classes). However, most users want to be able to identify the middleware by product name, so it is common practice to create one table for each product. From an industry perspective, if this was the approach taken for all CI classes and subclasses, you would end up needing hundreds of tables to cover hundreds of products, but in the case of middleware, you rarely find more than 6-7 middleware products that are most commonly used, especially in a single organization, so you can still manage with about 6-7 tables. The same scenario also applies for the virtualization platform. If the approach is to use the virtualization console as an MDR that provides details of all the physical, virtual and Based on our experience, we believe about 20 classes are adequate to build a CMDB in most organizations.

Once you have defined the classes (or more than likely – you have selected the classes you want to use from the list of predefined classes in the tool), you will need to define the attributes that you require. This is list of information that you want to hold for each CI class and the same equation applies- you will select the attributes from the predefined attributes. For example, for the server class, you will want to hold attributes like the hostname, amount of memory, location, description, SLA details, etc. It is easy to get taken in by the temptation to have many attributes for future use. This temptation leads to the overhead of filling in unwanted data – If you have a field, you will want data to fill it with and create unwanted burden on data maintenance. The cost of acquiring the initial data is far less than the cost of maintaining the accuracy of the data on an ongoing bases. Based on our previous experience, we believe about 25 attributes are adequate to serve the purpose of most organizations.

3.3.4   CMDB Ecosystem Design

The CMDB is a database that will hold information, but the design and architecture of the database must be designed with relevancy and sustainability in mind. The ecosystem design of the CMDB will depend on the data sources that will be providers of information for the CMDB, which are then further segregated as information may be imported from some via a manual upload, others may be integrated where data is updated on regular intervals, whereas data is federated from other sources. The architecture and design documents should be created at this stage.

It is important to understand the difference between "integration" and "federation" of data sources. Federation has evolved from integration. In integration, data is exchanged, while in federation, data is only referenced. Integration creates a copy of the data, whereas in true federation, the data remains in the original location and is queried, then represented on demand in the CMDB.

3.4   *Building Baseline*

An initial baseline of the CMDB would need to created, this provides a view of the snapshot of what exists in the environment and is a benchmark drawn for future references. The initial baseline creation is probably the most time consuming. Apart from identifying the data sources and actual collection of data for input into the CMDB, data validation and cleansing rules must also be defined to ensure that only validated and accurate information is populated into the CMDB.

3.4.1 Identify data sources

Based on the requirements collected during the planning and roadmap creation stage, the data sources would need to be identified for each of the different CI classes that are to be held in the CMDB. Several are logical data sources, e.g. network management tool for all network devices, discovery tools for infrastructure and application CI, storage management consoles for storage devices, virtual environment management consoles, etc. Most support groups also usually maintain spreadsheets for the components that they manage, which also form excellent data sources. Data validation for each data source may differ.

Non-traditional data source

Some tools, like event monitoring tools also form an excellent source of information, although these are not always looked at when considering sources of data for the CMDB. Yes, discovery tools would also provide the same set of CI's, however, in many deployments, tools like discovery do not get 100% coverage. This is not due to technical limitations, but due to other organizational policies. For example, discovery tools may not have access to servers in the DMZ, but to ensure that critical infrastructure is monitored so that issues are identified proactively, they are almost always monitored. Taking an extract from the monitoring tools and comparing it with the out from discovery tools (or any other data source that you are using for infrastructure CI's) could easily provide not only a validation of the information, but any CI's that may have been missed.

3.4.2   Data Collection

Data should be collected from the identified data sources. The thought of populating the CMDB overwhelms many organizations, because they want to store
every piece of data in the CMDB. While discovery tools take the hassle out of
manually collecting the data, they, too, can provide tremendous amounts of data,
not all of which may be required. Also, not every CI is appropriate for storage in
the CMDB; therefore, populating data collection can never be an entirely automatic, tool-driven process. Depending on the roadmap that you have created, not
all data may be collected at the initial stages, rather only the data that you intend
to import or federate from, so this may require filtering the CI's and attributes
that are required. An approach to simplify the process and to focus only on the
areas you need are to create "data collection templates", which map back to the CI
classes and attributes (fields) that you have in your CMDB. These templates should
then be populated in preparation to upload into the CMDB. This also works for
data sources that you are going to be integrating with and allows you to keep create
a "map" to link the fields in the CMDB to the data in your integrated data source.

3.4.3   Data preparation

Before data is uploaded into the CMDB, it will need to be prepared. Just import-
ing or extracting data from data sources and pushing into the CMDB is not
a good idea. The data source will likely hold lots of information that you may
not need as well as the same CI may also be provided by another data source.
You may also want to be selective and take attributes for a single CI from multiple sources. Also, depending on the data taxonomy, the data may need to be
transformed before it is uploaded into the CMDB. Ensure any data validation,
cleansing rules are run before it is imported into the CMDB. So effectively,
follow the ETL (extract, transform and load) approach. It is also important to
remember, that a single raw data source can become the data source for several
CIs or CI types in the CMDB, as in the case of the location data functioning as
an attribute of physical servers, firewalls, network devices, etc.

Similarly, although data "federated" sources is not imported, this may also require "mapping" so that the required data is queried and represented in the right fields and screens in the CMDB

3.4.4 CMDB baseline

Once the data is ready for population into the CMDB, it should be uploaded, data validated and tested. Any adapters to data sources that are being integrated, should be connected to the processing engine in the CMDB, transporting and loading the transformed data results into the CMDB.

When the data is brought into the CMDB, a "baseline" should be created, which provides a snapshot for future comparison.

3.5 CMDB Project Team

Any CMDB project team that wants to have a chance of successfully implementing the expected value from a CMDB will have at least four roles, namely a project manager, an architect, one or more technical consultant and a functional consultant. The architect will also be expected to have knowledge and experience of data models, taxonomies and will be supported by the functional consultant, who will be expected to have knowledge of how the data in the CMDB is to be used and referenced in the ITSM suite for the processes that consume the data. The responsibilities of these roles should be clearly segregated. A role can have multiple role players within the domain of that role. For example, there could be multiple technical consultants due to the use of multiple tools and technology components and you will probably not find one person who is an expert in every technology. Similarly, the project may turn out to be a program and in the project manager role you may have a program manager with multiple project managers. For example, if along with the implementing the CMDB, you also were implementing a discovery tool, which is quite common, they both may be run as separate projects, but under the overall program. Additionally, the requirement of a role does not imply that a person is required to work full time in the project.

Project manager

The project manager will own and manage the delivery of the CMDB project, ensuring that it is delivered to the required scope – within the agreed time and cost; not to mention, with the expected data in the agreed milestone phases.

The project manager is not expected to an expert on CMDB's, however having some previous experience of managing a CMDB project would of course be a huge advantage. The project manager will be expected to take input from the architect, technical and functional consultants to create the project plans with achievable milestones and a clear understanding of dependency on external groups/resources or even 3rd party suppliers to integrate into the CMDB to either provide or consume data from the CMDB. As with any project, there is always a risk of changing need and requirements, especially since stakeholders would have provided an ambitious wish list when gathering requirements, but when it comes to the implementation stage, it is not uncommon to find that the data expected to be available, is actually not. The project manager would be expected to manage the plans and expectations if such a situation arises.

The project manager would also be expected to ensure that the typical activities of any such project are formally managed, for example, documents for the design, architecture, processes, work instructions, handover to support, etc. are created, reviewed and signed off, report on the progress of the project as well as manage the resources, their allocation and time spent on the project and the overall P&L.

Architect

The responsibility of transforming the requirements for the CMDB into an architecture and design that can be used by the rest of the technical team to create the CMDB solution. This will include everything from implementing the CMDB tool, to integrating it with the MDR's or data sources, the methods to be used for integration also taking into account security and compliance requirements that have to be adhered to. The essence of the architect role is to create an architecture and design that will become the blueprint for the solution being implemented.

The architect is often looked at as the leader of the technical team and is expected to provide not only the initial architecture designs, but also oversee the team implementation life cycle. The technical team therefore needs to buy into and understand how the architecture developed by the architect is to implemented, in what stages, how the external data sources are to be integrated, how data is to be transformed, reconciled and how access is to be controlled when feeding information to other systems (data consumers).

The architect plays an important role in ensuring that the CMDB architecture aligns and adheres to the policy guidelines established by the enterprise architecture team.

Functional Consultants

A functional consultant (FC) is a business analyst for the CMDB, who will have a clear understanding of the expected content in the CMDB and its business purpose. The FC is expected to have analytical and conceptual knowledge of disparate data sets that could be structured or unstructured, complete or an incomplete part of the CMDB. The FC will have to deal with the challenges of large data sets in multi-tier environments. Having excellent data analysis and data management skills are vital for the FC as these are required to develop new ways of interpreting data and also to be able to scrutinize data from both the perspective of the consumer as well as the data provider.

The functional consultant will be involved in the planning, designing and oversight of the implementation and data population of the CMDB. They must thoroughly understand the requirements to which their design have to conform and how and where the data is going to be populated, maintained and eventually consumed. A degree of knowledge is necessary so that any necessary requirements are not omitted, or produce improper, conflicting, ambiguous, or a confusing structure. Functional Consultants must understand the various methods and solutions to design the CMDB.

The functional consultant can also double up as a process consultant to define the control and as well supporting processes for data maintenance, auditing, etc. If this is however not the case, additional process resources will be required to ensure that those aspects are also covered and the project does not become just a tool implementation.

Technical Consultants

The CMDB technical consultant will be an expert not only on implementing a CMDB, but also an expert on the specific CMDB tool that is being implemented. This usually is part of the ITSM suite and most technical consultants are skilled on implementing and configuring the other ITSM processes like incident management, change management, etc. This is an added advantage as they then also have an understanding of how the data is to be used by the other processes and therefore dependency on data taxonomies, categorization and the overall CMDB class and subclass structure. The technical consultant would be required to take the design created by the architect, along with the functional requirements from the FC to implement the CMDB. This will include integration with the external data sources and development of workflows to receive, reconcile, transform and upload data, where data is being replicated and populated into the CMDB. They would also be responsible for integration to external systems where data is just being referenced.

4 DISCOVERY

Discovery of CI's is an essential requirement for any successful CMDB project and anyone who has any experience of implementing a CMDB, cannot imagine doing so without discovery tools. In fact, most of the enterprises have acquired more than one discovery tools. The rule of thumb in most medium to large organizations is that if you were to collect all CI data manually, by the time you were finished collecting it, the data would already be out of date. Even if the organization was extremely disciplined and miraculously had all the CI records and attributes collected and maintained manually in spreadsheets, the identification of relationships between all the CI components and their dependencies would be almost impossible to gather manually.

However, although discovery tools probably provide the bulk of the information in the CMDB, they cannot discover everything. It is common practice to overlay the discovered data with manually collected attributes too. For example, once a server has been discovered, it will be further enriched with manual data regarding the SLA, criticality, environment that it operates in, etc.

4.1 Use of discovery tools in CMDB

Discovery tools serve two purposes in the building and maintaining of a CMDB:

1. Data discovery at the time of CMDB build: You will typically run a full discovery of your IT estate according to the CMDB data needs. There is lot of data processing steps before you actually load the data in the CMDB. These include normalization and reconciliation of the data.

Data normalization is when multiple data sources, like discovery tools, each name the same or similar attributes differently. E.g. "Microsoft" products can be named in multiple ways by discovery tools like MS, MSFT, Microsoft, etc. When data is imported into the CMDB, it is important that for this data to be normalized to a common format so that when a user is searching for the information, they do not have to provide multiple criteria or possibilities to look for a CI type.

Data reconciliation is when the same information is discovered by multiple discovery tools and data attributes are either selectively pulled for each tool (*e.g. the server host name from one tool and its model number and description from another tool*) and redundant and duplicate data is ignored.

2. For data maintenance, discovery tools again, can be used in two different ways

   a. Data update on the completion of a change: In this case you will usually run a targeted discovery on the specific IPs that are impacted by the change

   b. Audit and verification: In this case, you will, at regular interval, run discovery, and reconcile with the actual, CMDB and identify deviations and take corrective actions.

It is an extremely bad idea to run discovery tools and insert the data directly in CMDB. Discovery tools will discover lots of information, some that you may not want to keep, other data that is not captured in a user friendly format. It is common practice to clean up the data and only push selective information into the CMDB based on your actual requirements.

4.2 Basic Concept of Discovery

Trustworthy data is the foundation of the CMDB and the first step as well as the very core need is to create and maintain a baseline of the environment. The baseline is built with multiple data sources and the discovery is the primary data source.

Discovery provides the information related to **what exists** in the environment. There are a wide variety of discovery tools available in the market. Some are focused solely on a type of CI class while others are cross platform, discover different types of devices as well as software and applications. In our experience, discovery tools have a lot to be desired when it comes to discovering software. Understandably so. If you can imagine all the different software available in the market, it is difficult for vendors of these discovery tools to create signature patterns for each of them. However, there are some basic ways to at least identify what has been installed on a computer – be that a server or an end user device. Usually the way to discover installed software is via file scans, ARP/Registry, WMI and other probes and ISO tags. ISO tags are fantastic at delivering accurate data. The adoption of ISO tags is currently limited and progressing at a fairly slow pace. Discovery data used is most often used for populating the CMDB, but the same information can also be used for the purposes for managing software assets and licenses. There is difference between discovery for a CMDB and the discovery for Software Asset Management (SAM). In fact the discovery depth required for SAM is far less than that for a CMDB. SAM needs to know the one tier relationship – that is the relationship between the hardware and the installed software. It does not care about the relationship between two software CIs, for example relationship of application with database. However, for a CMDB the relationship between any to any CIs is an essential need. Similarly, the discovery for monitoring the managed objects of a CI is different than the discovery for SAM. The discovery needs and instrumentation for monitoring will depend on the object you need to monitor.

There are two methods of reaching out to the target system and fetching the data via discovery tools – agent based and agentless. The table below provides a comparison between both the methods.

Agent Based	Agentless
An Agent is physically installed on the device.	The agent is executed remotely on the device.
Admin access required for agents to be installed	Discovery can be done without admin privileges, however admin access will be required to run certain commands
It provides more in-depth information of hardware configuration and software installed	Information fetched depends on the probes and access rights provided
The Change Management process will need to be followed as the agent is being deployed	Less Change Management/build process concerns as no code is being deployed.
Consumption of system resources	No system resource consumption
Recommended for end user assets	Recommended for data center assets

Discovery can also be run in two modes – scheduled mode and on demand mode. The scheduled mode runs the discovery job and collects the data at the specified schedule that can be pre-configured based on the need and least disruptive times, for example in the middle of the night. This may work for data center devices, but will not work for end user devices which are most likely switched off at the time. Typically, even a monthly discovery would be good enough, but the frequency of running discovery would depend entirely on the rate of change within the organization and the maturity of the control processes.

Application Instrumentation and Discovery

Instrumentation defines how an application will expose itself for discovery. Windows Management Instrumentation (WMI) is the Microsoft application of the Web-Based Enterprise Management initiative for an industry standard for accessing management information. Most application vendors design adequate instrumentation for discovering their applications; however, you will find several applications not being discovered. Homegrown applications are the most likely candidates for such scenarios. If homegrown applications are not automatically discovered then this usually does not impact a legal compliance position as far as SAM is concerned, (you do not buy licenses - you are the full owner of the application) but this does impact the CMDB significantly more as you not be able to see the application and its relation to other CI's or the impact of an outage, etc. in CMDB.

Discovery considerations

Implementing discovery is often underestimated from a time, complexity and effort perspective. Technical experts who are responsible for the implementation, provide a time and effort estimate to create a plan, this also sets the expectation of stakeholders. However, although the information they provide is not incorrect, they usually focus only on the activities required to implement the tool and ignore the environmental and operational prerequisites. Agentless based discovery is desirable as it requires lesser effort to implement, however, this too needs to adhere to the security policies of the organization and from our previous experience, many departments in the organization need convincing before the required credentials are provided, ports opened on firewalls and approvals provided to run the discovery scans. All this takes time. Installation of agents is a big exercise in any organization, if this was the approach that was taken or if this is what the selected discovery tool requires. Then the actual deployment in distributed environment is time consuming.

Once these hurdles have been overcome, there is then of course the tool configuration to deal with. If you do not configure this efficiently, you will have an overwhelming amount of data to deal with. More data may be good, but not all raw data is required. It is important to avoid getting carried away with the tools capability and tempted to collect data that you will not use. For example, discovery tools will collect everything from security patches, operating system patches, etc., which are not always collected for a typical CMDB. On the other side you will also need to deal with the issue of incomplete data because the reach of discovery may not be 100%. For example, servers in the DMZ may not be reachable due to firewall and security restrictions.

Discovery output

After a successful discovery, you will have fairly good information about:

- What devices are deployed in the environment and in use

- How the devices are related

- Which software has been installed on which devices

- Who is using the devices

- How often they are used

Discovery limitations

Discovery tools cannot discover everything that you need to hold in the CMDB. There are technical limitations like target device or target CI instrumentation. Some devices like network security control devices and some storage devices are non-discoverable by most of the discovery tools. There are however management consoles provided by the vendors of these devices that can be imported into the CMDB or referenced directly.

For the devices and software that has been discovered, you will be required to add some additional data elements like their location, business owner, SLA, etc. manually. Location data becomes important for dispatched support – so that the technical resource knows where the device is physically located and also for software, if you have site licenses specific to geography.

Mobile devices discovery also lots of limitations because the technology is relatively new. However, Mobile device Management (MDM) tools are gaining maturity very quickly and discovery is an integral part of these tools.

4.3   Problems in discovery tool implementation

The biggest challenge in implementing discovery are actually non-technical in nature. Datacenter devices are governed by strict access and lots of security controls. Detailed discovery requires privileged access and that will require security approvals in any organization. Further, based on the network and discovery tool architecture, you will need to have some specific ports to be opened on the firewall to allow the discovery tool to communicate with devices that sit on the other side of the firewall. These are all manageable challenges but yet time consuming and require effort.

4.4   Problems in running discovery

Once the discovery solution has been implemented, running discovery scans do not always go smoothly. Some of the issues you are likely to encounter are:

- Credentials provided are incorrect and the tool cannot log into the server to run discovery. This is usually less for Windows servers as they are typically part of a domain and a single privileged account is required to access all these servers, this however doesn't work for non-windows servers (Unix) which may need an account created on the server specifically for the discovery tool

- Due to security or hardening of the server, the functionality to run certain commands (e.g. WMI commands on Windows server) is disabled and therefore discovery cannot identify the required information

- Ports on the firewall may not be opened and you will find once the scan has been run that the number of devices discovered is far less. The firewall issue becomes even more common with SaaS based discovery tools, which are then trying to come from an outside network over the internet to internal data centers and this makes the security department very uncomfortable. This can be overcome if the right architecture is deployed by placing a 'proxy server' for the discovery tool within the internal data center to perform the discovery and then pass it through to the central console over a single pre-defined port.

- The discovery tool itself will require lots of customization to write out sensors and probes to be able to run commands to discover exactly the information you need. This is more likely to happen when you need to discover specific software. Host and hardware information is typically easier to discover.

Again, all of the above issues are manageable, but end up taking lots of time and effort.

5 REMODELING EXISTING CMDB

Change is inevitable. What may have been fit for purpose a few years ago, may not be fit for purpose today. The business needs may change. No one can ignore the rapid rate at which technology is also changing. All of this will also have an impact on the CMDB at some point in time, warranting a remodel. Think of it as a remodeling of your home, which may have been designed as a bachelor pad when you were single and the only important events in life were social in nature, but at some point that same home may need to be remodeled to adapt to a new family member like a baby.

A remodeling may be required for several different reasons and the extent to you which you need to redesign and make changes to the CMDB may differ for each situation. In our industry, procuring services from external organizations is quite common. Services that have been internally provided may be outsourced to an external organization to achieve cost savings, flexibility of ramping up or down or even to make use of new technology or adopt cloud based services. This may therefore introduce a need for device based billing or internal cost charging to other departments, which will probably require holding additional attributes and data for each CI. It is also quite common in these situations to find the need for additional CI classes which didn't exist before – to adapt to new technology.

The requirement for remodeling may even impact only a particular class of CI. For example, if a new virtualization technology was being introduced in the environment, it will introduce a need to integrate or reference the MDR for this virtualization technology. So a new integration is required. This will then require some reconfiguration within the CMDB and a revisiting of the data model to ensure that the imported/referenced data can be made available to users in the right format and in the relevant fields, screens and forms.

The scope of the CMDB will also not always stay static. It is common to expand the scope of the CMDB over time. Most organizations start populating the CMDB with the easily discoverable devices, like servers and then once this has been completed, expand the scope to include software, applications, business services, etc. All of this may require remodeling. As the other CI's are to be populated, it is also likely that new discovery tools will be implemented to support capturing these CI's. It is normal to find multiple discovery tools, capturing the same devices. This will then require you to build reconciliation rules to make sure that you do not create duplicate devices just because they are discovered by multiple tools. The scope may also change to incorporate a radical change in features or functionality within the ITSM tool or other processes that consume data from the CMDB.

Another fact that cannot be ignored – the CMDB is a tool, in almost every case, this is a commercial off the shelf tool sold by a vendor, rather than developed in house. All vendors will come up with new versions of the tool and at some point, stop providing support for earlier versions. The upgrade does introduce new structures within the CMDB to support the ever changing technology landscape. When an upgrade of your CMDB tool is performed, this will always require a revisiting of your CMDB structure, data model, attributes and workflows.

You will find that you need to audit and clean up your data over time. It is important to note that cleaning up of the data held in the CMDB, whether this be removing redundant information to filling in missing data, is not remodeling.

When you do need to remodel your CMDB, the areas that you would typical look to restructuring or redefining would be:

- The taxonomy

- The CI classes and subclasses

- The attributes that you hold for the CI's

- Integrations with external systems or MDR's

Data transformation to reconcile or change the value of imported data before it is populated in the CMDB

Remodeling because of tool Change

This is a common scenario. Many CMDBs are built in ITSM tools and an organization may choose to change the ITSM tool. In such cases, the CMDB would need to be remodeled according to the new tool. This would require the remodeling of the data model and practically a new CMDB built. However, significant efforts of data collection, data validation and data preparations would be eliminated as the existing CMDB could be the sole data provider for the CMDB base lining in the new ITSM tool.

You may also require re-engineering the process for configuration management to keep the CMDB current.

Remodeling because of migrating CMDB to ITSM tool

Some organizations may have built the CMDB outside of the ITSM tool and may want to migrate it to the ITSM tool. Practically, the approach would be the same as if you are changing the tool, but for the need of process engineering.

When you build a CMDB in the ITSM tool, several control processes for data maintenance are embedded into the ITSM tools. If, originally the CMDB were outside the ITSM tool, the control processes would also be outside ITSM tool and in such cases, on migration, new process will be required in the ITSM tool.

6 CMDB ACCURACY

CMDB accuracy means the data you hold in CMDB is error free. The value of the CMDB lies in its accuracy and it is the most important utility attribute of any CMDB. Therefore maintaining the accuracy is meeting the purpose of the CMDB. To achieve a reasonable level of accuracy (good enough to serve the business purpose) is not impossible, although it is difficult. How difficult is it? The answer depends on the volume of data, the type of data (structured, unstructured, source etc.) and the desired level of accuracy. Why it is difficult has both technical and non-technical reasons. In the world of IT everyone understands technical difficulty and limitations and those generic technical difficulties are applicable here too, although there are technical solutions for those issues.

Non-technical difficulty is generally ignored (or deliberately ignored?) We believe, in many cases it has to do with the organization's working culture, value system and the typical attitude of solving every process problem with technology. Every piece of work in life cannot be done with a tool. There are manual inputs in the CMDB too. People just do not want to put in the effort and always expect some tool to be made available. Thomas Carlyle, a famous Scottish satirical writer, once said, "Man is a tool-using animal. Nowhere do you find him without tools; without tools he is nothing, with tools he is all." Yes, he is right, and definitely for people in the IT industry. Tools make life easy. If something can be easily done with a tool, then make that tool available. But do you need a calculator to calculate 2+2? There are many things that can be done easier and faster without tools and there are things that can be done at a lower cost with manual efforts. With CMDB data maintenance, manual update would be inevitable.

Yet another aspect of non-technical difficulty is the failure to budget the operational cost of maintaining the CMDB or the absence of willingness to spend on operations. If you do not have the funds required for a CMDB to be implemented and operated - do not expect a professional outcome.

Now let us compare this situation with a similar situation in financial management of any business organization where check payments are routinely released to suppliers, while the business also routinely receives the money from customers. These issued payments may not have been debited to or credited from the bank account at a single point in time, so the actual monetary position of the business will be different to what is reflected in the bank account. However, the CFO and the finance department of every organization are fully aware of both, the cash position and the bank position of available balances at a reasonable and workable accuracy. The primary reason is

1. No money is paid or received without being recording in the books

2. Account books are regularly audited and reconciled

Why can't we have the same kind of discipline in IT operations? Why do IT folks tend to do things that impact the business without recording it? I was once conducting a workshop to implement demand and release management processes. When I explained the importance of demand, I talked about the best practice of recording a demand and delivering it through the release management process. I noticed that the general practice in the organization was to receive application enhancement request by e-mail, fulfil the work without any accountability. The staff argued that this was good customer service.

My question was- what will happen if a user requested for an expense to be reimbursed by e-mail to the accounts department. Naturally, I was told that this would require submitting a proper receipt in the prescribed template. So even if the user need to put in a $50 claim they would have proper recording, an entitlement policy and complete accounting backed by a comprehensive process. However when an enhancement that requires 8 hours of a developers time (cost $800), there is no accounting!! We need to quit this gung-ho cowboy attitude.

6.1 Accuracy Defined

Accuracy can be defined as the ratio of correct data elements in the database and the total data elements, represented as a percentage, at a given point in time.

- Data elements that are in scope must have a well-defined, agreed and scoped values for system performed data validation

    - For example, selection values, date values, etc.

- Free text data elements such as the description of CI's, summary, etc. are not in scope for accuracy calculation

    - System generated or discovered data is in scope, even though it could be text data (host name or audit trail for example)

Examples of data elements that are typically considered to be in-scope when calculating the accuracy of a CMD are:

- Hostname – though free alphanumeric values, but included in scope because it has defined unique value

- IP address – Cannot take any arbitrary value and the value can be validated for a predefined format

- Patch level - in scope because each product patch level can have a defined value

- Deployment date: database supports date field natively

The accuracy of the CMDB can vary with time. Attribute values change, for example the value in the CI business owner field - people join or leave the organization or even change roles, but this data may not be changed immediately. Data that is discoverable is easier to update. Data that is manually maintained is more likely to cause the accuracy of the CMDB to vary.

6.1.1   Inaccuracy by design

A CMDB can be designed to be inaccurate – if you are adding fields for which the data cannot be maintained or is difficult to maintain, then you are compromising the accuracy by design. Port addresses for an application or port number of a firewall are example of the data element that are typically difficult to maintain within a short update frequency cycle.

Below is an illustration of measurement:

- The CMDB has 1000 servers, and each server has 25 attributes, of which 20 attributes are in scope

  - If the patch level in all the servers is missing (not populated) then accuracy is 95% (1000 data elements incorrect out of 20,000 data elements)

    - if no value is entered, it is counted as an incorrect value

  - If the patch level is populated for all the servers, but incorrect in 50 servers, then the accuracy is 97.5%

Missing data can be deemed as an "incomplete" CMDB, but we would like to include missing data in the calculation of inaccuracy.

6.1.2 Accuracy vs completeness

There is a difference between accuracy and completeness. As discussed above, when we look at the accuracy of the CMDB, we are typically looking at the data that is held in the CMDB and if that data is accurate. Yes, we do include missing data attributes into this calculation. Completeness, on the other hand, looks at the CI records in the CMDB.

To better explain this, let's look at an example. If there were 1000 servers deployed in the environment, but only 900 servers recorded in the CMDB, this would be 90% complete. Completeness is the ratio of "expected" records and the actual records in the database. This is typically calculated for complete CI records, rather than attributes of a CI record.

Since the number of "expected" CI's is hypothetical, the measured value of completeness will also be hypothetical at any given point of time. Completeness can be predicted on the basis of historical data of missing CI discovered in a period of the time.

6.1.3 Example of incompleteness by design

A CMDB can also be designed to be incomplete. For example

- If the CI attribute for "business owner" is missing in the data model, but it is deemed as required information in the CMDB, then the CMDB would be incomplete by design

- If this field is available and not populated, then even though it is missing information, we would consider it in the measurement for accuracy, provided this field is in scope for accuracy calculation

It is quite common for organizations to define SLA's for the CMDB, especially when this service is the responsibility of an external supplier. It is usually provided by the infrastructure service provider. An arbitrary, but high number is usually agreed and included in the contract. The definition for accuracy is rarely defined and agreed and no party ever discusses, agrees or highlights if the CMDB is actually designed to be accurate and if the data maintenance processes are adequate enough to keep it accurate or if the CMDB will by design be inaccurate.

6.2   Need for accuracy

The whole purpose of a CMDB is to be a data provider to support other processes. If you cannot trust the data you are presented it, there is little point in collecting and maintaining that data. It is a waste of time, effort and money. Inaccuracy is a death knell for the CMDB.

If you needed some data to make a decision and that data wasn't available, you will likely call and check with someone who knows more about it before you make your decision, or, you will guess. If you were to guess, you will know that you are making a decision based on a guess and know that there is a risk. If you know there a risk, you will hopefully, have some mitigation in place if your decision turns out to be incorrect. However, if you were provided inaccurate information and didn't know about it was incorrect at the time of making your decision, which is even riskier as you will not have made any provision for mitigation.

Accuracy is something that has to be worked on right from the beginning and across the entire data that is held in the CMDB. If you have been impacted by incorrect data once, no matter if the rest of the data is accurate, the next time you have to rely on the information in the CMDB, you will probably not trust it.

6.2.1   Cost of Accuracy & completeness

There is a cost associated to having complete and accurate data in the CMDB. It takes time, effort and therefore funds to initially collect data and then to keep it accurate. This is why, we keep talking about building a sensible CMDB and only collecting and maintaining data that you need, rather than collecting everything that you can discover or find. It is difficult, but vital to not be tempted into hoarding information just because you may find some use for it sometime in the future.

The cost for accuracy and completeness is directly proportional to the number of CI classes, number of CI records and the number of attributes each CI record contains. The more the data, the greater the cost, as you will need to do more work.

An argument that we have heard on several implementations is that the discovery tool will gather it anyway, so how does it matter. This is not entirely true. Yes, discovery may find information that you do not necessarily need or want, but if you do decide to hold it, it will more than likely require data normalization, reconciliation, inclusion in audits and supporting processes to keep it updated with additional manual data overlaid to make it fit for use.

The total cost of ownership will include both project build and the ongoing operational costs to maintain the data. It will also include things like storage, computing resources to normalize and reconcile data, so although tempting to hold more than you need, it is crucial to keep asking yourself if the data is really needed and what it will be used for. Some supporting processes to main the data can be automated, but not all process can be automated. They will require time and effort from several different groups and resources to ensure it is both complete and accurate.

6.2.2 Measuring Accuracy

The purpose of an audit of the CMDB is to identify:

- If the CI records held in the CMDB do actually exist in the environment

- If all the in scope CI's that exist in the environment are also reflected in the CMDB

- If the data held in the CMDB for the CI's is in fact accurate

The audit can be conducted in several ways. The approach you take will depend on several factors like if you are trying to do a full audit, a particular CI class and also if the information you are trying to audit is discoverable or not. The complexity will be compounded by the amount of data you actually hold in the CMDB.

The typical methods used to perform an audit and identify incorrect information in the CMDB are:

- Running a full discovery and comparing the results with the data held in the CMDB

- Picking a small percentage of random CI's from each CI class to verify if the non-discoverable data held for those records is accurate. Although this will not give you a full audit result, it will give you a good estimate of the accuracy for those attributes. It is possible to do a full audit for non-discoverable attributes too, but based on the amount of data elements, this can be very labor intensive and time consuming

- Doing a physical audit (manually check servers in the DC) for a small subsection of CI's. Rather than identify identifying CI's from the CMDB, you can approach it from the opposite direction and randomly pick CI's in the environment and verify that they do exist in the CMDB with accurate information from both discovery tools as well as the manually maintained data

- Check change records from the last audit for a random set of CI's to verify if the updates are reflected in the CMDB

- Compare the CI records with a non-traditional data source, for example the monitoring tool to check against the list of records held in the CMDB match.

6.3   Audit

We are often asked how frequently an audit of the CMDB should be performed. There is no wrong answer and it would depend on several considerations. In many CMDB implementations that we have been involved in, the deployment and maintenance was being provided by an external service provider. As you can imagine, every service provided by an external supplier usually attracts some form of an SLA, which is normally reported on a monthly basis, some quarterly. It is quite common to come across contracts which ask for "accuracy the CMDB" as an SLA to ensure that the supplier is committed to keeping it up to date. In this case, the audit should be provided at least quarterly, to ensure that the SLA performance being reported on is verified.

Considering that an audit may be performed on a quarterly basis, it isn't really feasible to perform an audit of every single data element. It more than likely will not be completed within the 3 month window, before the next audit has to start. The more pragmatic approach is to pick 5% of the CI records from each of the classes, or even the key CI classes and audit those. Even within those 5% records, you do not need to audit every single attribute, you can pick the key attributes from both discoverable and non-discoverable data elements and audit those. We have provided some methods to consider in the section above.

What happens if you were to find inaccurate data? Will that percentage be then extrapolated to the rest of the CMDB, even though all of the other information may be completely accurate? Unfortunately, until the entire CMDB and every data element is audited, you will not get an accurate picture, but then is that really required? As long as a valid portion of the CMDB is audited – one that provides a large enough sample that provides a conclusive result of the findings and one that you feel confident of making corrective decisions based on. The sample size would typically depend on 4 variables:

- Total data elements:
    - o CI classes that are in scope, total CI records in each class, number of attributes for each class

- Degree of accuracy required

- Degree of confidence required

- How often you expect your audit criteria to be met

Simple random sampling is an example of a probability sampling method. It should result in your sample being representative of the characteristics of the whole CI class, due to random selection reducing the possibility of any systematic bias that would make the selected records different in character from the overall CI records. To ensure representative results this method should be used in conjunction with a calculated sample size.

Strictly speaking, a sample size calculation should be carried out for each audit criteria that is being addressed as part of your CMDB audit. The sample size chosen for your project should be the largest figure that those calculations produce.

The table below provides a guide to choosing an audit sample sizes and assumes an expected incidence of 50% i.e. that standards will be met 50% of the time. It gives the sample size you will need in order to be 95% sure (degree of confidence) that the results you obtain from the sample will be within 5% (degree of accuracy) of the results you would have obtained for all your CI records if you had collected data on all of them. Put another way, there is a 1 in 20 chance that your results will not be representative.

Total CI Records	Sampling Error	Confidence Level	Max expected error rate	Sample Size
1000	2.00%	95%	5.00%	313
1000	2.00%	90%	5.00%	244
2000	2.00%	95%	5.00%	371
2000	2.00%	90%	5.00%	278
5000	2.00%	95%	5.00%	418
5000	2.00%	90%	5.00%	304
10000	2.00%	95%	5.00%	436
10000	2.00%	90%	5.00%	313

You will notice that the sample sizes need to be proportionately smaller as the total number of CI records increase; looking at 418 out of 5000 records giving you results with the same degree of certainty as looking at 318 out of a total of 1000 records. This is because the chance of the results being unrepresentative is dramatically reduced as the total size increases. This should however be sampled across a CI class rather than different CI records from every class. This is because if you are discovering and maintaining the location of CI's, but haven't maintained the business owner field, then including them both in the random sampling will not give you the desired results.

To increase the accuracy, the approaches you take at the time of building the CMDB and maintaining it during steady state operations will be slightly different. At the time of building the CMDB, you will focus on getting your discovery tools to identify all your CI records and then also gather, collect, collate to upload additional information that cannot be discovered. However, during the steady state operations, the focus will not be around full discovery, but to ensure that the control and support processes are adhered to and any missing information is added.

6.4 Data maintenance

Theoretically speaking, once your CMDB has been implemented, if there are no changes to the environment at all on an ongoing basis, the accuracy of your CMDB will remains as it was when it was implemented. This typically would be quite high, because when engagements like this are run as projects, they typically have the attention need, the funds, the resources and the collaboration of everyone involved. However, your environment staying static with no implemented changes is not possible in any IT operations. It can however be assumed that if the CMDB is properly maintained through a strictly adhered to change management process, the CMDB accuracy would still be achievable and stay at the same level. However, from a practical point it is very difficult to achieve this because of the following reasons:

- Controversial as it may sound, we can safely say that the IT professionals are not the most disciplined and their laziness to record and update information results in issues with maintaining the accuracy of the CMDB

- In appropriate use of discovery tools to maintain the CMDB

Our species was defined as "Man the Tool Maker." The use of tools is undoubtedly a fundamental characteristic of man. However, tools cannot solve process problems. They can help enforce, automate and support processes, but you need to define the process that the tools have to follow. A fool with a tool is still a fool. Ensure "rule before tools"

Who owns the data in the CMDB and whose responsibility is it keep it updated or correct it when inaccuracies are found? We rarely tend to look at other parts of the organization for inspiration to solve our problems, but there is a lot that IT can learn from the HR or finance departments. How does HR maintain accurate employee records for payroll and tax purposes? You will never find them paying an employee who has left. If issues are found in employee records, who initiates the correction for it? Another excellent example is the finance department. How do they always know the exact cash position, when checks are being issued for payments, funds are being received and the incoming or outgoing is not happening at the same time? Data maintenance for the CMDB can learn a lot from these two departments.

6.4.1   It is Futile to solve process problem with tool

Data input into the CMDB can be automated. Data sources can be either integrated, federated or referenced. The rules for the import, data normalization and reconciliation can be pre-defined. The audit criteria, comparison rules and results can also all be pre-configured. But the key thing to note is that the rules, workflows and processes to both input data into the CMDB and then maintain that data have to first be defined, before this is configured in the CMDB. Most organizations assume that by buying tools, they are actually somehow receiving and implementing processes. If you look at this practically, tools are designed by vendors, to be sold to as many organizations as possible. They are developed to perform a function, where the vendors believe there is a gap or issue in the market. But at the end of the day, they are developed to be sold to as many organizations as possible. They have to be able to support process guidelines provided by ITIL, MOF, custom processes or in some cases – no process at all. So out of the box, they do very little. They will only deliver the desired result once you have defined your process and then configured the tool to automate or enforce it.

7 MAINTAINING CMDB

Whatever you build requires maintenance. So does the CMDB. You will come across two areas of maintenance with the CMDB:

1. Maintenance of the data or content to keep it accurate and current

2. Maintenance of the data model and taxonomy

Configuration management deals with both; additionally tools and process maintenance will be the self-serving in configuration management.

7.1 *Configuration Management process*

The ITIL definition of the configuration management process is about *identifying and defining the Configuration Items in a system, recording and reporting the status of Configuration Items and Requests for Change, and verifying the completeness and correctness of Configuration Items.* In other words, it is an end-to-end process for building, maintaining and operating the CMDB. So far we described the CMDB building process. In this section we will discuss maintaining the CMDB.

In an ideal world, once a CMDB is built, the only event that should change data in the CMDB is the execution of a request for change (RFC). Therefore, you could maintain the currency of the CMDB, if you can somehow ensure the update reflected in the CMDB on the successful execution of every RFC (we will discuss how complex this "somehow" could be later in this section.) Change management is often called the gatekeeper for the configuration management process because any update in the CMDB should be done via the change management process. Thus it is important that any change that includes changes made to configuration items have tasks created for updating the CMDB. In the real world however, there are two practical scenarios

1. Your CMDB is likely to have data that is not under change control. For example, the roles associated with a CI (business owner of a CI, technical owner of a CI, etc.)

2. There will be unauthorized or unregistered RFCs and you will not be able to guarantee the update for those changes

To address the first scenario, you must have additional control processes to update the data. This data is most likely to be non-discoverable and the control processes unlikely to be fully automated.

To address the second scenario, you should have some mechanism to detect and remediate unauthorized changes. This remediation could either be rolling back of unauthorized changes or regularizing the change and updating the CMDB. This mechanism is actually part of the audit process and must have formal prior agreement and be institutionalized. CMDB reconciliation tools and configuration audit tools facilitate this audit.

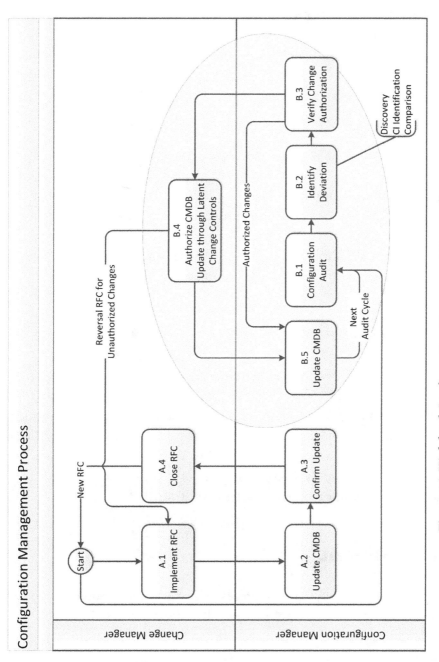

Figure 16: High level Configuration Management Process flow

It is important to note that although at a high level, all CIs are controlled via the change management process, however at a procedure level; the activities for configuration control may differ for each type of CI based on multiple factors like:

- Availability of a discovery tool for that class of CI

- Population of non-discoverable Cis, their attributes and relationships

- Availability of alternate sources of data

Under certain circumstances (like updating non-discoverable attributes), the request fulfilment process can also be used for configuration control.

Verification and audit processes will differ based on availability of discovery tools and other reliable sources of CI information.

7.1.1 Implement RFC

This is shown as activity A1 in the process. As part of the requirements for logging an RFC, the CI on which the change will be performed must be related to the RFC. Other relationships may also be made; for example, to an incident or problem. Post implementation of the change, there may or may not be a requirement to update the CMDB, depending upon the scope of the CMDB. It is the responsibility of the change implementer to engage configuration management to reflect the required updates in the CMDB.

7.1.2 Update CMDB:

This is shown as activity A2 in the process. If a change to a CI requires an update to the CMDB, the change implementer will perform the CMDB updates, after the implementation of the change. The configuration management process ensures that no CI is added or modified without the appropriate control-ling documentation. For example, an approved RFC is associated with the CI impacted by the related change. The update could either be manual or through discovery tools.

Manual Update:

The CMDB should allow manual update for non-discoverable CI and attributes.

Manual update of limited records

If a change is implemented which has altered the attributes of a limited num-ber of CIs in the CMDB, then the CMDB can be updated manually to reflect the updates in the CIs.

Listed below are some of the scenarios wherein the CMDB can be updated manually:

1. A new CI introduced in the environment

2. Change in the attributes/configuration of an existing CI

3. Update in the CMDB as a corrective action or exception post CMDB verification & audit

Manual Update of Bulk Records

Manual update on bulk records permits user to modify attribute(s) and relationship(s) for multiple CIs simultaneously, thereby speeding and simpli-fying maintenance of the CMDB.

Following are some of the scenarios wherein CMDB can be updated manually:

1. Servers migrated to a new data center location, which results in site attribute to be modified in multiple number of servers

2. An owner name needs to be replaced in large volume of CIs

Discovery Based Update

CMDB can also be updated using information from discovery tools. Discovery scans will typically be configured to run at two distinct occasions:

1. Targeted discovery

2. Scheduled discovery

Targeted discovery scan:

If the modified CI is discoverable through discovery tools, then the CMDB administrator will perform a targeted CI discovery to populate and keep the CMDB current after completion of the change. Target discovery is nothing but scanning a specific IP address or range, which was part of the change while avoiding scanning any other IP range.

Full discovery scan:

Complete discovery scan of the environment is usually performed on a periodic basis (preferably monthly or quarterly) on the entire datacenter subnet ranges. This ensures the CMDB is consistent with the physical state of CIs and identifies any unauthorized changes.

7.1.3 Confirm Update

This is shown as activity A3 in the process. Post updates to the CMDB, the CMDB administrator will send a delta report containing the new specifications and the status of the CI, which would in turn assist change management to validate if the desired outcome has been obtained as a result of the implemented change. If an update to CMDB was to add a new CI, then CI technical owner must also be informed to provide any non-mandatory attributes.

7.1.4 Close RFC

This is shown as activity A4 in the process. Change management will use the delta report to validate if the changes made to the CI are in accordance to the approved CR and matches with the desired state of the CI. This will also identify any incorrect manual updates to the CMDB due to human error. If there are any discrepancies, then remediation activities must be undertaken, which might result in a corrective or roll back RFC. Post verification, the change can be moved ahead to the closed status.

7.1.5 CMDB Audit

This is shown as activity B1 in the process. The purpose of the audit is to identify the CI existence or accuracy of the CMDB. Audits should verify that correct and authorized versions of CIs exist in CMDB. Any unregistered CI should either be removed or registered through formal change control process. Unauthorized CIs/attributes that are discovered during configuration audits should be investigated and corrective action taken to address possible issues. The configuration manager is accountable and responsible to carry out audits, publish audit finding and seek updates on the corrective actions.

Two distinct forms of audit will be performed at agreed interval

- Audit for discoverable CI information – This will be performed using discovered data from full infrastructure discovery scan or a manual inspection of random sample.

- Audit for non-discoverable CI information – This will be performed using random sampling

7.1.6   Identify Deviation

This is shown as activity B2 in the process. To audit the CI details within the CMDB, the first assessment to be made is based on the total number of CI's within the CMDB versus the total reported in the audit data. This initial assessment is to ensure that all CI data within the CMDB has been correctly authorised.

Where the total number of CMDB CI's does not match the total provided by the audit data, investigation is required and issues and corrective actions identified as appropriate.

CMDB CI's greater than audit data

Where the CMDB CI total is greater than reported by audit data it is likely that service management processes to update (decommission) CI's within the CMDB have not been performed correctly.

Audit data greater than CMDB CI's

Where the audit data total is greater than recorded as CI's within the CMDB it is likely that service management processes to add (commission) CI's within the CMDB have not been performed correctly.

Verify CMDB CI attributes against audit data

Along with verifying the CI count, the CI attributes must also be audited. The set of attributes associated with each CI Type to be verified should at least consist of all mandatory attributes, whereas non-mandatory attributes are discretionary.

Audit data and the attribute details within, will be classified as follows:

- Automatic source of truth – audit data attribute is automatically generated and is not impacted by manual update processes (e.g. discovery tools).

- Manual source of truth – audit data attribute is manually generated but is classified by the service provider/customer as the primary source of such data.

7.1.7 Verify Change Authorization

This is shown as activity B3 in the process. As a result of the audit, if any gaps are identified, then the configuration manager must perform a comparison between the CI and the authorized RFCs, which are implemented in the past. If there is no corresponding RFC to the changes made to the CI, then it would be deemed unauthorized and non-compliance to the change management process.

A delta tracker developed based on the audit findings will be communicated to the CI custodian and to any identified beneficiary parties. The configuration manager is accountable and responsible on developing the delta tracker. The report will consist of a list of unauthorized CIs and a tracker to capture the actions taken to resolve the inconsistencies. CI custodian will be responsible to investigate and drive the audit findings to closure.

7.1.8 Authorize CMDB Update through Latent Change Controls

This is shown as activity B4 in the process. In order to record the changes made to a CI, a retrospective or a latent change will be required as per the change control process. If for any reason, the CI needs to be configured back to its previous state, a change needs to be submitted to perform a rollback.

7.1.9 Update CMDB

This is shown as activity B5 in the process. In case a change is rolled back, a corresponding update to the CMDB will be done as a part of rollback change request.

7.1.10 Data model and taxonomy maintenance

The data model, once designed will not usually change, provided the design is done with future considerations. At least the class and sub class would not change. There may be some additional fields or taxonomy addition requirements from time to time. For example, if your classes are product based and you introduce a new product.

7.1.11 Tools and process maintenance

Tool administration and support is generally understood well and planned adequately, but process maintenance is rarely understood well. Actually, processes breakdown more often than the tool. In our first book "Process Excellence for IT Operations" we have discussed this in detail.

7.2 Automation of data maintenance process

Do not solve a process problem with a tool

I have encountered many CMDB implementations where the automated discovery and uploading of the data directly into the CMDB is completely automated. Feeding of data into CMDB directly without reconciliation and authorizing against approved changes is a faulty concept. This approach of update deletes the trace of unauthorized changes in the environment. There is no argument with the need of automation in the data maintenance process but the *"rule before tool"* policy must prevail. Reconciliation of the actual data with the authorized data is an important part of the data maintenance and reconciliation can largely be automated. The reconciliation process is discussed in next section. The Verification activities in reconciliation may not be fully automated- rather not feasible or cost effective automation.

7.2.1 Reconciliation Process

The reconciliation process has three steps - identify data from multiple data sources, compare that data to information stored in the CMDB, and merge it with CI data stored within the CMDB. When creating a full picture of a CI, gathered from different data sources, you want to make sure that all attributes are associated with the correct CI.

Reconciliation is the process we use to resolve similar identifying characteristics. The identity management system, for example, "reconcile" different identities to the same or different people based on identifying attributes such as name, birthdate, SSN, employee ID or domain ID. Similarly, for reconciliation each CI needs identifying common attributes such as its host name, MAC ID, system generated CI id, asset tag etc.

"Identify" is the phase where a CI gets identified on the basis of a unique combination of various attributes and a unique reconciliation ID gets assigned to the CI record in any of the logical data source datasets. In this phase it is also determined whether the information contained in multiple logical datasets refers to the same CI. A unique identifier is CI information that distinguishes one CI from another in any logical dataset. Identifiers are critical to identifying data across multiple data sources; it is also key to identifying similarities between discovered data and the data that is stored within the CMDB in the "Authorized CMDB" dataset.

"Compare" is the phase where a comparison is done in between the "Authorized CMDB" logical dataset and CIs that actually exist in the environment.

As an outcome, the compare phase creates a list of differences (deltas) between production (Authorized CMDB) and a sandbox CMDB logical datasets. There would be various scenarios while receiving CI data from multiple data sources that a specific attribute is authorized to be picked from one data source while another one is authorized to be picked from another data source. For example, "Memory" discovered by discovery tool A is authorized, but the "IP Address" discovered by tool B is authorized.

Reconciliation engines' "Attribute Preference" table help in building an attribute preference set for a specific CI class utilizing finalized business rules that maps a specific attribute value to a specific data source. The output of compare is a deviation list – the difference between actual values and recorded value of CI attributes.

The final phase in the reconciliation process is "Merge/Update CMDB", where the qualified deviations are updated into the CMDB.

Workaround for reconciliation

Most of the ITSM tool providers offer some form of reconciliation capability or engine along with their ITSM product but not all vendors have this offering. Some vendors have a workaround feature. This feature allows you to create a CMDB baseline through discovery and then compare the baseline with newly discovered data. It will point out a deviation but not point out exactly what has changed. You will need to manually investigate the nature of the deviation.

7.3   CMDB Operation team responsibilities

Just like we have defined the roles for the project team during the building of a CMDB, this section looks at the operational roles. One role may have multiple resources depending upon the size/volume and type of data in your CMDB as well as quality and accuracy requirements.

Data Model Maintenance

This role ensures that the data model is maintained and kept fit for purpose. There will always be changes in the environment with the adoption of new technology as organizations try to achieve more at a lower overall cost. This could drive a redesign of the data model or even an upgrade of the CMDB tool may initiate this. Some of the key skills required to maintain the data model are strong analytical skills, knowledge of how the data in the CMDB is used by other processes, knowledge of how the tool is structured and the impact that data model amendments will have not only on future upgrades to the tool, but what data mapping will be required to discovery tools or MDR's used to populate the CMDB. The resources would also be expected to have good documentation, design and architectural skills.

Key responsibilities include:

1. Understand and adopt changing business needs into the data model

2. Work with the technical development teams to implement data strategies, build data flows and data model updates

3. Create logical and physical data models using best practices to ensure high data quality and reduced redundancy

4. Optimize and update logical and physical data models to support new and existing projects

5. Maintain conceptual, logical and physical data models along with corresponding metadata

6. Develop best practices for taxonomy used and standard naming conventions used to ensure consistency of the designed data model

7. Validate business data objects for accuracy and completeness.

8. Analyze data related integration or federation challenges and propose appropriate solutions

9. Develop data models according to organizational and approved architectural standards

10. Review modifications to CMDB tool upgrades and its impact on the data model

Process maintenance

This role ensures that the processes are working as designed and that there is no bug in the process. The process efficiency and effectiveness, as well as continual improvement is the main focus of process maintenance. Data maintenance is not the responsibility of process maintenance.

Key responsibilities include:

1. Work with the tools administration staff, CMDB administrator and configuration manager to optimize the rules relating to infrastructure discovery, reconciliation jobs and promotion of the updates to the golden or production data set in the CMDB

2. Expand the functionality, scope and accuracy of the CMDB by analyzing feedback from operations staff

3. Devise configuration management audit schedules, tools and offer governance for the procedure of correcting identified deviations along with identification and implementation of preventive actions

4. Educate the service delivery teams regarding the benefits of using the configuration management procedures and that of relating incidents, problems and changes to specific CIs

5. Help the configuration manager in identifying management information that would be useful for planning technology and architecture refresh projects

CMDB Librarian/content management & Reporting

This is very data intensive role. The main purpose of the role is to ensure that all CI records are accurate and contain consistent information. The focus of this role is to ensure the integrity of the CMDB and to account for, manage and protect the integrity of CIs through the service lifecycle by working with teams including change and release management to ensure that only authorized changes are made to enable service management teams to make informed decisions.

Key responsibilities include:

1. Maintaining the integrity and accuracy of the CMDB through regular audits and reconciliation reporting.

2. Assisting in the documentation of configuration management policies and procedures.

3. Complying with the configuration management process.

4. Assisting in the development of training documentation for the use and maintenance of the CMDB.

5. Analyzing reports and statistics to ensure consistency, performing changes and updates as requested.

6. Develop and maintain on-going monitoring and reporting of anomalies relating to change activities.

7. Measure and provide quality analysis on the impact of changes to configuration items and their related application and business services

8. Preparing and executing bulk data uploads and evaluating data to maintain data and system integrity

9. Provide reporting to measure the utility and warranty of CMDB

Tool administration and support

The skills required to perform this role are primarily technical in nature. The resources would be expected to be experts on the tools/technology used for the CMDB. This is more likely to be part of a large ITSM suite, so the technical resources would also likely need to understand, support and administer the overall ITSM product used. Once the tool has been implemented, focus is mostly on administration, but there would also be upgrades implemented on a periodic basis, additional or new requirements, new data sources integrated, new federated sources, so the technical staff are also needed to have development capabilities to be able to perform these activities. If not, they may be managed as a project with external skills brought in as required. Discovery tools may also be supported and managed by the same team, so resources may be cross skilled if possible, or a certain person(s) focused solely on the administration and support of the discovery tool.

Key responsibilities include:

1. User Guidance:

    a. Guiding users on usage of the CMDB as required

    b. Review and updating documentation as a result of any development or configuration changes to the tool

    c. Supporting users involved during user acceptance testing including provision of user test cases

    d. Training to the user community on new roll-outs

2. Data Configuration

    a. Making changes to the data model, CI classes, sub classes and attributes

    b. Creating new relationships

    c. Uploading manual data (bulk uploads) as required

    d. Maintenance of user access rights and views, e.g. to modify or create CI's

    e. CI additions, modifications and deletions

3. Support management:

    a. Resolve any incidents or requests related to the CMDB and discovery tools

    b. Liaise with the tool vendor for escalated issues

4. Integration and data sources:

   a. Maintain integrations to data sources and MDR's

   b. Add new data sources

5. Development:

   a. Upgrade the CMDB and discovery tools

   b. Continuous improvement with building new functionality, work-flows and automation

8 SERVICE MAPS

B efore discussing service maps, it would be worthwhile to discuss about service architecture.

Service Architecture

What is a service? It is essentially the set of benefits realized by the execution of a set of activities by a function/person or by machine(s)/configuration item(s) or by both. Service architecture is a logical and conceptual model of a service describing service properties and realized by the data model. A complete service architecture would include all of the following:

1. Service Functionality/Outcome

2. Service chain entities

3. Service Economics

4. Service Consumption components

5. Service Usage and Billing

6. Self Service Components

7. Service Support components

8. Service security components

9. Service Monitoring and control components

In traditional service management service maps are sufficient for the purpose of service management, but in the XaaS (Everything as a Service) era, all nine elements listed above are necessary for service management.

Service architecture is also important for cloud service management. We intend to write a separate book on cloud service management where we shall elaborate this point further.

Service Maps

A set of service producing CIs form the service map/physical model of service that is a subset of the service architecture.

A **service map** is a graphical representation or the topology of a service that illustrates how the service is built using various components. These components generally include hardware, software and their relationships. All of the data to build and show the service maps is stored in the CMDB. Many organizations try to add configurable settings or roles, as well as customers and other services to the service map, but based on our previous experience, that kind of a system would be a very complicated build, which most organizations would struggle to implement. The purpose of a service map is to gain an understanding of the service's structure to allow managing it effectively. A service map is not the only thing that is required to manage the service, the associated roles, configuration settings and other attributes are also required to determine how the service is delivered and controlled, thereby ensuring expected availability, capacity, security, and manageability.

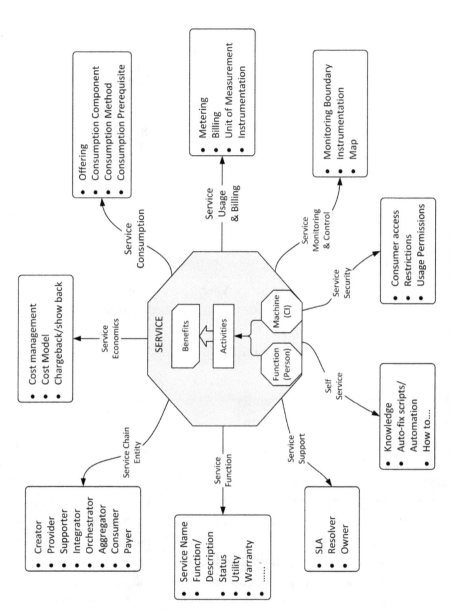

Figure 17: Service Architecture for XaaS Environment

Service maps bring a lot of value in documenting an environment because they

- Present a service-centered view of the environment;

- Create a bridge between technology and the business by organizing technical capability in business oriented terms;

- Facilitate understanding of complex systems and component dependencies.

However, service maps should not be seen as a substitute of end-to-end information at a micro level. The following table explains what a service map is and what it is not:

Service map is	Service map is not
Abstracted information of the structure of a service that is derived from multiple sources, including service design documents such as an architecture overview A map for navigation to determine the impact of a component on the service	A replacement for service design documents, such as an architecture diagram Recorded in a service portfolio or service catalogue

Service maps support processing of event management data by providing information on the structure and dependency of a service for correlation and impact analysis of events. Service maps today are implemented with various differences across the many tools used, which leads to major chaos in reconciling and identifying authoritative sources. Service maps are core artifacts not only to help manage the business service but also for integration of services in a multi-service provider environment. Service Integration and Management (SIAM) is gaining momentum in the ITSM world and will continue to get more attention as organizations outsource services to multiple vendors and until the dependency of the components and knowing which supplier is responsible for it is clearly understood, it will be extremely difficult to manage.

There are three methods through which organizations can build service maps today using tools available in the market:

1. Use CMDB discovery to create service maps and then import them from the CMDB in an event management tool—this approach will become irrelevant in a dynamic IT landscape as discovery tools are scheduled and not real time. (Run time service modeling is the answer to this where you create a separate RTSM database with different set of tools. RTSM is discussed later in this book)

2. Use application transaction models to discover service dependencies—this approach is application down but leaves out the details of the infrastructure elements.

3. Use native discovered data by element managers and create service maps at the event management tool level—this approach ensures that authoritative sources feed the service maps. The key issue to manage is the integration of data models from different tools, which can lead to complexity.

Service catalogue, CMDB, and service maps

A **service catalogue** is the published list of all services in production. A service catalogue is a subset of the service portfolio. A record in a service catalogue will include key service attributes. The CMDB is the database of all configuration items. A CI record will show the key attributes of a CI. A service map will use the CMDB and service portfolio data to illustrate the structure of the service and its relationships with different CIs. The below is a simplified diagram, however, one business service may contain one or more IT services

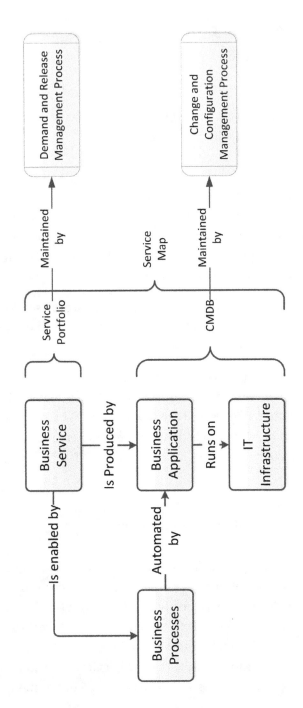

Figure 18: Service Map and CMDB

A service map provides an end-to-end view of how the service is built using various components. These components generally include hardware, and all kinds of software, such as databases, middleware and applications software and their relationships. A Service map provides great help for managing the end-to-end service. The purpose of a service map is to gain an understanding of its structure and the interfaces and integrations in the end-to-end service. Service maps define how the CIs are bound together for each specific service. Service map is the service-oriented view of CI integration map. Service maps provide the information about the interfaces and integrations points. There is a lot of misconception in the IT user community about service maps being automatically built by discovery tools and data feed to CMDB. Most ITSM tools provide some capability to build and use service maps but the amount of time and effort required to build and maintain service maps is very high. Unfortunately, vendors create an illusion that it is extremely simple and a relatively quick job while selling or overselling the capabilities of their tools.

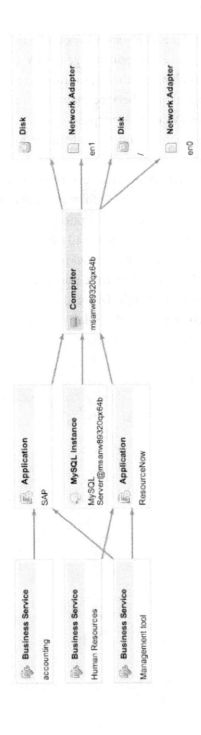

Figure 19: Example of Service map (source- wiki.servicenow.com)

8.1 Service Maps and BSM

Vendors use BSM in their marketing messages and always relate it to the strengths of their own products. BSM is not just a product; it is a methodology that is enabled by multiple products and, more importantly, a set of service management processes.

A true BSM system will enable a set with the following functionality:

- Understand the enabling business service by IT

- Map it to the underlying configuration items within IT infrastructure

- Maintain the maps that are dynamically changing (possibly real time; but all tools do not support real-time map maintenance)

- Monitor and manage end-to-end service by monitoring and maintaining the state and performance of CIs using an appropriate set of processes and tools

BSM is a layer above IT service management and IT service management must be mature enough to support BSM. Similarly, application performance management (APM) is about monitoring the applications related managed objects such as the application processes and transactions, linking them to business services through service maps, determining the business value, and then delivering rapid, proactive problem identification and triage to help resolve problems before they impact end users and critical services.

The selling point of application performance management is that it allows IT organizations to be in control of the customer experience by enabling them to proactively identify, diagnose, and resolve problems before end users and revenue generating services are affected, while assuring consistently high service levels that meet the demands of business. In other words, both buzz-words mean a comprehensive combination of event management process plus CMDB, plus service maps and run time service models in action.

OMDB (Operation Management Database) in figure 16 is actual a CMDB that is not reconciled and includes additional data related to the dynamic state of virtual infrastructure that the CMDB will not include. The foundation of the CMDB and the OMDB is the same technology. The OMDB provides operational data like downtime, alerts, SLAs and data related to availability and performance management for service modeling tools to build RTSM (Run Time Service Models). RTSM primarily serves event management.

1. Drive event processing on top of a dynamic, near-real-time model of the IT infrastructure.

2. Correlate various monitoring sources against managed services to provide a comprehensive view of the health of the service

3. Serve as a central repository for dynamic changes discovered during the course of real-time operations to facilitate the cases above.

A BSM toolset includes OMDB and modeling tools. The foundation of successfully implementing BSM are:

- Service Maps

- A mature event management process

- Implemented capabilities for event detection, filtering and qualifications, correlations and control response to events

- Mature, accurate and current CMDB, with the right depth

- Mature set of all ITSM operational processes

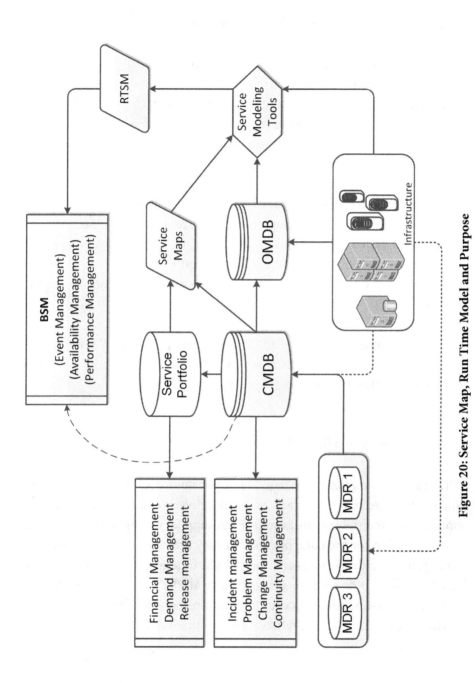

Figure 20: Service Map, Run Time Model and Purpose

8.1.1 Service Maps vs Run Time Service Model

Let us go back to the analogy of CMDB/Service maps with Google maps. A Google map is static. You can search for a location, get driving directions, print those driving directions and follow them to reach your destination. When you use an application to navigate, the intelligence in the application may start with one route but these applications have the capability to suggest and dynamically change the route depending on the traffic and road conditions. Similarly, run time service models represent the service map in real time. The snapshot of a runtime service model is a service map at that point in time. Intelligent infrastructure consists of load balancers, and automated migrator tools like vMotion (in VMWare) in virtual environments that can dynamically move guest OS instances to clustered hardware based on utilization and change the service map depending on the workload.

The most prominent example of an OMDB is available in the VMware environment. vCenter Server 4.1 database has 39 tables providing all the three databases – CMDB, OMDB and service maps.

8.1.2 Service Maps for SIAM

Within a multi supplier ecosystem, the responsibility for support of IT components that are reliant on each other to deliver an end to end service is spread across multiple organizations. Each supplier manages and maintains the information for the components that they are responsible for. The customer procuring the services and their SIAM function do not automatically have the ability to discover or easily identify all the components in the service delivery chain, but are accountable and responsible for the end to end service. In this situation, the reliance on a mature CMDB with service maps is even greater.

Service delivery integration

To really understand how a service is built up, which components provide and support that service and from an operational point of view – which supplier to contact when things do not work, it is vitally important for the SIAM organization to build a CMDB with service maps. The service maps are a core capability that is required for the SIAM function to be able to perform its duties. It provides them with a graphical view of the service (top down), along with the information of who owns the service, who supports the components, the agreed SLA's and other operationally vital data. If they don't understand this, they cannot integrate the suppliers or manage the services.

Service transaction map

Industry has yet to talk about transaction service map visualization- we discussed this in our Service Integration book for operation integration vs service map for service delivery integration.

Unified Command center as a part of SIAM

The SIAM function is responsible for operationally integrating the multiple suppliers in the environment and ensure that a seamless end to end service is delivered. The SIAM function works extremely closely with the service desk as well as the command center, which is responsible for monitoring and event management. This combined function makes integration of services seamless and drives common metrics and visibility on operational data which makes day to day working less about sentiment and I believe this vs you believe this and more about operational data driving incident and problem resolution. An 'unified' command center which captures business impacting alerts, visualize the service dependency from the service maps and react on them in advance of the end users realization that something is not working is the optimum operating model. This would also enable common reporting and ability to provide a single view of performance across all service providers and help to achieve the operational alignment and robustness needed for the function to succeed.

Benchmarking of delivery capabilities

The business always wants the highest SLA's. This may not always be possible or cost effective. Services have to be designed and architected to meet the required and agreed SLA's. When service level requirements (SLR's) are gathered, these need to be verified against the delivery capability to meet the requirements. This gets more complex when the services are delivered by external and multiple suppliers. The CMDB and service maps play a vital role to enable validation and confirm if the services are architected to meet the requirements, if not they should renegotiated, or the services should be redesigned.

8.1.3   Service Model for Event management Process

An event can be defined as any detectable or discernible occurrence that has significance for the management of the IT Infrastructure or the delivery of IT service and evaluation of the impact a deviation might cause to the services. Events are typically created by an IT service or a CI. If you have had any experience with monitoring tools, you will be aware that they can and do generate thousands of alerts when implemented out of the box. The tools have to be configured to make it meaningful for your purposes and only generate events for the parameters that you are interested in and when certain thresholds are met. To really make event management work for you, events also need to be correlated. Event correlation is a technique for making sense of a large number of events and pinpointing the actual issue that you need to work on. This is accomplished by analyzing the relationships between the components that generate the events. To look at a simplified example, if 5 servers were connected to a switch and the switch went down, event monitoring tools would typically generate and display 6 events. One to show that they switch was down and then another five to show that the servers were unreachable. Now, if you didn't understand the topology and relationship between the components, support staff would have diagnose all six events, but when the events are correlated, the tool is able to understand and tell you that in fact, you only have the one event to deal with, which is the switch being done. This is based on the network topology, which can be derived from the network topology discovery tools. But, using traditional discovery tools or network topology, you would not be able to discover services, this is where service maps and the CMDB come into the picture. Now, if you were to take correlation one step further, to understand the impact of events on services, which is really what the business cares about, then that is where the CMDB would play a vital role. The information and mapping of infrastructure and applications to services is done in the CMDB, which can provide the information to the event management process. The impact can be measured both top down and bottom up. For example, if a server was part of a cluster and it were to go down, although event management would show that as a critical issue, the service would not be impacted as it would continue to function on the secondary node of the cluster. Similarly, if a load balancer had stopped working, event management would not show the underlying infrastructure or applications as down, but the service would be impacted and would cease to work. Service maps and the CMDB also provide the event management process the information that it needs to really be effective.

9 BUILDING SERVICE MAPS

As shown in the figure 15, you would need to build a service portfolio and the CMDB to build service maps.

9.1 Service Portfolio

The service portfolio contains current services being offered, future proposed services as well as retired services. It also includes third-party infrastructure or applications services that form an integral part of the service offerings to customers.

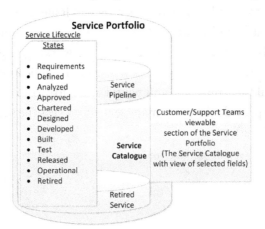

Figure 21: Service portfolio and service catalogue

Service portfolio versus service catalogue

The service portfolio is divided into three sections: service pipeline, service catalogue and retired services. Services should be clustered according to lines of services based on common business activities they support. Only active services should be visible to customers/support teams.

A service portfolio is focused on information required by the business, whereas the catalogue provides a view of the consumable components or request-able items. If we refer back to "Figure 17: Service Architecture for XaaS Environment", all of the attributes listed under the nine elements would be held in a common store and some elements only visible in the portfolio for example. cost management, charge back/show back, billing, etc.), some elements only visible in the catalogue, while others like the support group, resolver group, etc. only visible in the CMDB. There would of course be lot of attributes like the service name, description, etc. that would be visible in all of the views of the portfolio, catalogue and CMDB.

9.1.1   Design

The service portfolio should be designed in a manner that helps identify the services, based on what they deliver or comprise of. The service categories and sub categories should clearly align the services based on similar objectives, whether it is a common business goal or the services are constituted of a similar composition. For example, core differentiator services can be a service category and the sub category can consist of manufacturing business function systems such as payroll or a benefits portal; or utility services such as a network or server farm can be grouped together.

The following factors also need to be kept in mind while designing the service portfolio:

1. Service Name: The service should be depicted in business terms instead of in technical terms. It should be clear what the service is aimed towards providing so there is no ambiguity towards what the service is named and what it actually delivers. E.g. "email" can be a service but MS Exchange should not be named as a service as it is only a component which is be used to support the email service.

2. Business Functions: Identify the business processes and functions that rely on and are supported by the service.

3. Service Investment: Explain and document the investment in the service and the contribution of the service to the organization in terms of lower costs, competitive advantage, or regulatory support.

4. Business/Service Sponsor: A business unit manager should be identified who directly supports the IT service through financial commitments. This is mandatory, as going forward the business/service sponsor approval will be required in order to enhance or retire the service from the portfolio.

5. Roadmap: Information about future planned upgrades, release, possible replacement or decommissioning should be captured. It is recommended that a roadmap for the next two- to three-years should be included in the Portfolio.

9.1.2 Defining Service portfolio

Service Naming Convention

The naming convention used for service needs to aim at standardization. In our experience, most organizations lack a naming convention or standards and this leads to each system developing and providing services in isolation of the other, instead of relying on a centralized or enterprise managed approach. A very common malpractice across different organizations is to use an application as a synonym with a service. A service is independent from the applications which support it. A single application can also be used to support more than one service.

Naming conventions should remain consistent throughout the organization as this increases the potential to reuse, leverage and achieve integration channels with individual services in a more easily recognized manner.

Data Model & taxonomy

A model should be drafted of what a service is expected to achieve and acts as a justification for the investment into that service by describing the potential benefits, resources, and capabilities required to develop and maintain the service.

Taxonomy for services should be clearly defined and a standard naming convention should be used to ensure uniform vocabulary. This will also help produce a consistent service catalog, which will have the same meaning to every customer in the market/industry.

Templates

A structure needs to be established in the form of templates to collate and consolidate data pertaining to the interdependencies of applications, infrastructure components and data in order to provide the desired service.

A uniform structure is important so that if there are any modifications to the service in a later release, then the new/modified data would be collected in the same format to maintain consistency.

Who can provide data?

The primary data provided for the portfolio is the application team, as they are the single source of information of current or upcoming applications and services. The other sources of information can also be the PMO organization. Many organizations also have a group of people who are part of IT, but manage the relationship with the business and play the role of a business service manager. They would also be a good source of information for upcoming services or changes to existing services.

9.1.3   Mapping with CMDB

The CMDB is built bottom up and most of the underlying infrastructure is identified using discovery tools. Discovery tools also manage to identify databases and several commercial off the shelf applications. Signature patterns for custom applications will need to be configured in the discovery tool so that they too can be discovered. Tools however do not realize what service or environment each of the discovered clusters of connected devices actually are. They are not able to identify the user friendly names organizations give each of the service or what business process and service they support. The tools do however provide an outline of the connected CI's, including identifying the relationship. The service CI's are typically created manually in the CMDB and then manually mapped to the discovered cluster of connected CI's.

9.1.4   Publishing

Once the content of the service portfolio has been identified and documented, it would need to be published so that users and stakeholders in the business can view and access it. The functional design of the portfolio is quite an important criteria and addresses requirements around who can view it, the required access control, what content is available to which users, easy navigation, etc.

9.2   *Portfolio maintenance*

The portfolio is managed by the demand and release management processes in the same way as the CMDB is managed by change and configuration management process. Once the portfolio is published, there will be two events that will require an update-

1. Business requesting enhancements: Services are actually enhanced by application enhancements. For every application enhancement demand, a feature will be added in the application and consequentially in the service. This will warrant a modification in the service attribute or the modification in existing service record. The enhancements are deployed through the release management process; therefore release management is the natural point of control for any portfolio updates.

2. Business requesting a new service: New services are actually project requests and the point of entry is demand management. This will again be released through the release management process and warrant an addition of a new record in the portfolio. The record should be entered in the portfolio as soon as the demand is approved (status of service – chartered) and when the release is deployed, then the service status becomes operational

9.3   *Project and operation Roles*

Just like the CMDB, building and maintaining of service portfolio will also require project and operation roles. However, the size and complexity is much smaller. Listed below are the roles that would be expected in both the build/ project and the operate phases. The skills, activities and key responsibilities of these resources is similar in nature to the ones listed in section3.5 and 7.3, although the focus is the service portfolio rather than the CMDB.

Project Roles

- Project manager

- Functional consultant

- Technical consultant

Operation Roles

- Process manager

- Portfolio manager

- Technical administrator

10   ANNEXURE: CMDB TOOLS AND AUTHORS VIEW

"**M**an has many tools at his disposal, but is always on the quest to acquire new ones". This has been the evolution of Man since the stone ages, to keep inventing tools. But the success of these tools is greatest when they are simple, meet a purpose and are effective to use.

In relation to collecting information about all the components that make up an IT environment, the first generation of tools were focused solely on asset management. These later took on the semblance of a CMDB. This was achieved by adding relationship capabilities but at the core were asset management tools and mostly supported those models and lifecycle. We tag them as CMDB impersonators.

The second generation of CMDBs came with pure CMDB data stores, which were underpinning ITSM transaction systems and were mostly built on extensions of the DMTF CIM Model. These CMDB tools had some value at a point in time but would need continuous reconciliation from their own native discovery sources to be updated and stay relevant. In Parallel we had application performance management (APM) tools, business service management (BSM) service map tools, systems monitoring tools that all claimed to have a built in CMDB but were in essence providing a limited view of the entire landscape.

Many of them did have a more accurate operational model of the services than traditional discovery tools. These tools couldn't solve the purpose of a CMDB to the full extent. This was also the case with configuration management tools which held the current configuration state of the devices which were managed by their agents, but they gave a partial view of the entire landscape. Even identity management or directory systems had the human view/CI data and systems like MS Active Directory staked a claim into the CMDB world.

In the technology market for CMDBs, there have been many such evolutions on the capability, functionality and flexibility of tools. In the 21st Century Enterprise and as per the various examples and models that have been discussed in this book, our opinion is that the more infrastructure is deployed in a model driven or blueprinted approach, the gap between the design time and runtime would become negligible. The operational database (OMDB), which is based on the current state of the environment and would become the source of "operational truth", while the CMDB would become the ground truth in terms of holding "The Map". We see the CMDB in its true sense as a "Graph Model" which would store information regarding the Service Maps across a hybrid enterprise. We also see the OMDB evolving using extensive machine learning and graph algorithms to be able to process real-time service models from various sources and be continuously referencing the Service Map for the greater benefit of the Enterprise. We see Asset Management as being a completely independent and separate data model which shouldn't be muddied by mixing it up with CMDB and causing unnecessary confusion.

11 GLOSSARY OF ACRONYMS AND ABBREVIATIONS

APM	Application Performance Management
ARP	Address Resolution Protocol
BMC ADDM	BMC Application Discovery and Dependency Manager, previously called *Tideway*
BSM	Business Service Management
CAPEX	Capital Expenditure
CFO	Chief Financial Officer
CI	Configuration Item
CIM	Common Information Model
CMDB	Configuration Management Database
CMDBf	Federated Configuration Management Database
CMS	Configuration Management System
CR	Change Request
DB	Database
DC	Data Center
DIKW	Data, Information, Knowledge and Wisdom
DMTF	Distributed Management Task Force
DMZ	Demilitarized Zone
DR	Disaster Recovery
DSL	Definitive Software library
ELA	Enterprise Licensing Agreement

ERP	Enterprise Resource Planning
ETL	Extract, Transform and Load
FC	Functional Consultant
FRU	Field Replaceable Unit
IOT	Internet of Things
ISO	International Organization for Standardization
IT	Information Technology
ITBM	Information Technology Business Management
ITIL	Information Technology Infrastructure Library
ITSM	Information Technology Service Management
KPI	Key Performance Indicator
LMDB	Landscape Management Database
MDM	Mobile device Management
MDR	Management Data Repository
MOF	Microsoft Operations Framework
MS	Microsoft
NOSQL	Not Only SQL (structured query language)
OMDB	Operation Management Database
OPEX	Operating Expenditure
OS	Operating System
PMO	Project Management Office
RACI	Responsibility, Accountability, Consulted, Informed matrix
RDBMS	Relational Database Management System
RFC	Request for Change
ROI	Return on Investment
RPC	Remote Procedure Call
RTSM	Run time Service Model
SAM	Software Asset Management
SAP	SAP SE (Systems, Applications & Products in Data Processing) is a German multinational software corporation that makes enterprise software to manage business operations and customer relations
SAP SLD	SAP System Landscape Directory

SIAM	Service Integration and Management
SKMS	Service Knowledge Management System
SLA	Service Level Agreement
SLR	Service Level Requirements
SQL	Structured Query Language
SSN	Social Security Number
VM	Virtual Machine
WMI	Windows Management Instrumentation

ABOUT THE AUTHORS

Prafull Verma

Prafull Verma has a bachelor's degree in electronics and communication engineering and has over thirty years' experience in the area of electronic data processing and information technology. He started his career in India in the area of electronic data processing systems and later moved to the United States in 1997. During the past thirty years, he has worked on diversified areas in computer science and information technologies. Some of his key experience areas are the design and implementation of heterogeneous networks, midrange technical support management, end-user service management and design, and the implementation and management of process-driven ITSM systems.

Prafull has acquired a unique blend of expertise in integrated areas of tools, process, governance, operations, and technology. He is the author of several methodology and frameworks for IT service management that include multi-vendor ITIL frameworks, ITSM for cloud computing and Service Integration.

Prafull's competencies and specializations include the area of merging engineering with service management, as this book manifests, and outsourcing business management.

Currently, Prafull is working for HCL Technologies Ltd., Infrastructure Service Division, and Cross Functional Service Business Unit, as Fellow and Chief Architect. He is also serving member of the product advisory council of ServiceNow, the industry leading ITSM platform.

Mohan Kewalramani

Mohan Kewalramani has over 15 years of experience in IT service management transformation projects, ITIL consultancy, process re-engineering and ITSM tool deployments.

Mohan spent the early years of his professional career in the Middle East, before moving to the UK in 2007 and has worked with customers all over the Middle East and Europe. His knowledge goes beyond the theoretical and he prides himself on having implemented the realistic, practical and efficient, including implementations in multi-supplier environments with cross delivery processes, interfaces, including tools and technology to support service and systems management and has led large service management projects, several of which have been to implement CMDBs with varying degrees of complexity including some in a multi supplier outsourcing environment.

Mohan is employed with HCL Technologies Ltd., Infrastructure Service Division, and Cross Functional Service Business Unit, as Associate Director and Global Head of the Service Integration and Management Practice.

Kalyan Kumar

Kalyan Kumar (KK) is the Chief Technologist for HCL Technologies – ISD and leads all the Global Technology Practices. In his current role Kalyan is responsible defining Architecture & Technology Strategy, New Solutions Development & Engineering across all Enterprise Infrastructure, Business Productivity, Unified Communication Collaboration & Enterprise Platform/ DevOps Service Lines. Kalyan is also responsible for Business and Service Delivery for Cross Functional Services for HCL across all service lines globally.

Kalyan is widely acknowledged as an expert and path-breaker on BSM/ITSM & IT Architecture and Cloud Platforms and has developed many IPs for the company in these domains. He is also credited with building HCL MTaaSTM Service from the scratch, which has a multi-million turnover today and a proprietary benchmark for Global IT Infrastructure Services Delivery. His team is also credited with developing the MyCloudSM platform for Cloud Service Management & MyDevOps, which is a pioneering breakthrough in the Utility Computing and Hybrid Agile Ops Model space. He has been presented with many internal and industry awards for his thought leadership in the IT Management space.

Kalyan also runs the HCL ISD IPDEV Incubator Group where he is responsible for incubating new services, platforms and IPs for the company. He is also active in the Digital Systems Integration Roadmap and Solutions Strategy for HCL. He has also co-authored a Book **"Process excellence for IT Operations: A practical guide to IT service Management" (http://tinyurl .com/k7u3wyf)** and two more books are in pipeline of being published

Kalyan has spoken at many prestigious industry platforms and is currently actively engaged in Partner Advisory Board of CA Technologies, IBM Software etc.

In his free time Kalyan likes to jam with his band Contraband as a drummer / percussionist and reviews Consumer Technology Gadgets and follows Cricket Games Diligently. Kalyan lives in New Delhi, India with his family.

KK can be followed on Twitter @KKLIVE and at Linkedin (http://www.linkedin. com/in/kalyankumar).

FROM THE SAME AUTHORS

Process Excellence for IT Operations: a Practical Guide for IT Service Process Management

Authored by Mr Prafull Verma, Authored by Mr Kalyan Kumar B

List Price: $29.95
6" x 9" (15.24 x 22.86 cm)
Black & White on White paper
332 pages
Process Excellence for IT Operations
ISBN-13:   978-0615877525   (Custom Universal)
ISBN-10: 0615877524
BISAC: Computers   /   Information Technology

As the title suggests, the book is providing a practical guidance on managing the processes for IT Services. There are lot of guidance available on technology management in IT industry but this book is focusing on technology independent service management. The book will be addressed to all IT people from a process practitioner perspective, however, the fundamentals are presented in simplistic terms, and therefore it should be useful to all IT people. It will describe the process engineering concept and how it can be applied to IT Service Management. This is not about the industry standard framework such as ITIL and COBIT but about the common processes that are generally used in real life operations. This book does not focus on any technology.

Foundation of IT Operations Management: Event Monitoring and Controls

Authored by Mr. Prafull Verma, Authored by Mr. Kalyan Kumar

List Price: $15.95
6" x 9" (15.24 x 22.86 cm)
Black & White on White paper
138 pages
Foundation Of IT Operation
ISBN-13:   978-0692205709   (Custom
Universal)
ISBN-10: 0692205705
BISAC: Computers   /   Information
Technology

In IT operations, event monitoring and control - where you continuously monitor the health of IT infrastructure and take proactive measures to prevent the interruptions in IT services- is dominated by tools and technology but there is a meticulous process behind it. This book tries to demystify the underlying process for this kind of operation management. There are lot many books on service management but those books do not cover this subject adequately and leave this area to be addressed by tools and technology. Tools vendor on the other hand, focus on the tool part, leaving the process aspect to the service management professionals. This book fills in the void and connects both, the process and the tools to provide a holistic view. The book takes an educative tone and written primarily for IT generalist and not for the tool experts, although it would give a new perspective to tool experts also.

Service Integration: A Practical Guide to Multivendor Service Management

Authored by Prafull Verma, Authored by Kalyan Kumar

SERVICE INTEGRATION

List Price: $15.95
5.5" x 8.5" (13.97 x 21.59 cm)
Black & White on White paper
148 pages
Service Integration
ISBN-13: 978-0692219959 (Custom Universal)
ISBN-10: 0692219951
BISAC: Computers / Information Technology

This book is intended to present simplified guide for IT generalists who are new to the service integration subject. The purpose of this book is to educate all IT professionals with the basic concepts of the service integration. Additionally the purpose is to provide the core guidance and foundation guidance to Service Management professionals, upon which they can build and implement the service integration in their environment.

Software Asset Management: Understanding and implementing an optimal solution

Authored by Mr Prafull Verma, Authored by Mr Kalyan Kumar

List Price: $15.95
6" x 9" (15.24 x 22.86 cm)
Black & White on White paper
148 pages
Software Asset Management
ISBN-13: 978-0692324264 (Custom Universal)
ISBN-10: 0692324267
BISAC: Computers / Information Technology

Software asset management (SAM) is an essential need for all IT organizations, not just because of the cost of software but also because of the potential litigation of copyright violation for use of unlicensed software. Most of the organizations deploy tools for software asset management, but fail to achieve the desired goals because tools are a small part of the holistic solution. This books explains the underlying complexity of SAM and includes all aspects of SAM solution that includes solution architecture, the SAM processes, tools and function and provide a guideline to develop, build and operate an optimal solution

www.ingramcontent.com/pod-product-compliance
Lightning Source LLC
Chambersburg PA
CBHW071157050326
40689CB00011B/2148